Oxford International Primary Maths

Tony Cotton

Caroline Clissold

Linda Glithro

Cherri Moseley

Janet Rees

Language consultants:
John McMahon
Liz McMahon

6

OXFORD
UNIVERSITY PRESS

OXFORD
UNIVERSITY PRESS

Great Clarendon Street, Oxford, OX2 6DP, United Kingdom

Oxford University Press is a department of the University of Oxford.
It furthers the University's objective of excellence in research,
scholarship, and education by publishing worldwide. Oxford is a
registered trade mark of Oxford University Press in the UK and in
certain other countries

British Library Cataloguing in Publication Data
Data available

978-0-19-839464-8

3 5 7 9 10 8 6 4

Paper used in the production of this book is a natural, recyclable
product made from wood grown in sustainable forests.
The manufacturing process conforms to the environmental
regulations of the country of origin.

Printed in Great Britain by Bell and Bain Ltd, Glasgow.

Acknowledgements

The publishers would like to thank the following for permissions to
use their photographs:

Cover photo: Patryk Kosmider/Shutterstock, P30: Matt Slocum/
Associated Press, P83: inan avci/OUP, P101: Shutterstock, P121:
Hemant Mehta/India Picture/Corbis/Image Library, P130: Dreamstime.
com, P149a: Matteo Festi/Shutterstock, P149b: Steven Mayatt/
Shutterstock, P149c: Shutterstock, P149d: Fotolia, P149e: Martin
Bech/Shutterstock, P149f: Mayovskyy Andrew/Shutterstock, P149g:
Andrey Armyagov/Fotolia, P149h: Shutterstock.

Although we have made every effort to trace and contact all
copyright holders before publication this has not been possible in all
cases. If notified, the publisher will rectify any errors or omissions at
the earliest opportunity.

Links to third party websites are provided by Oxford in good faith
and for information only. Oxford disclaims any responsibility for
the materials contained in any third party website referenced in
this work.

Contents

iv

1 Number and Place Value

1A The number system

Discover

Complete this table using the correct script. If you know any other scripts complete the final column.

Hindu-Arabic (European)	Arabic	Bengali	Cantonese	
37				
	٢٤			
			七十一	
58				
			三十五	
	٧٢			
43				
			六	
		২৯		
		১০০		

Write 6 different number sentences below using scripts that you do not usually use. You should include 3 addition calculations and 3 subtraction calculations.

I. _____   4. _____

2. _____   5. _____

3. _____   6. _____

1A The number system

Explore

Imagine you visit a planet inhabited by aliens like the ones pictured. Invent a number system that they might use. You should invent words for the numbers 1–20 and symbols for the numbers 1–100

Complete the tables below using your invented number system.

One	Two	Three	Four	Five	Six	Seven	Eight	Nine	Ten

Eleven	Twelve	Thirteen	Fourteen	Fifteen	Sixteen	Seventeen	Eighteen	Nineteen	Twenty

1B Place value

Discover

Place value game

	Millions	Hundred thousands	Ten thousands	Thousands	Hundreds	Tens	Units

- Use a set of 0–9 digit cards.

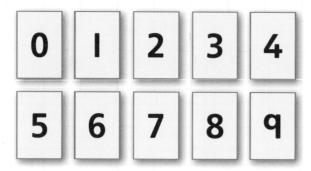

- Choose a card.
- Write the digit in a column in the grid. (You cannot change this at a later stage.)
- Replace the card.
- Choose a card again.
- Write this digit in a column in the grid.
- Repeat until all the spaces are full.
- Now complete the following in words:

  The largest number was

  _____

The largest possible number with these digits is

_____

The smallest number was

_____

The smallest possible number with these digits is

_____

The number nearest to 5 million was

_____

The number nearest to 5 million possible with these digits is

_____

The number nearest to 8 million was

_____

The number nearest to 8 million possible with these digits is

_____

- Repeat the place value game:

	Hundreds	Tens	Units	Decimal point	Tenths	Hundredths
				•		
				•		
				•		
				•		

- Now complete the following in words:

The largest number was

_____

The largest possible number with these digits is

_____

The smallest number was

_____

The smallest possible number with these digits is

_____

The number nearest to 10 was

_____

The number nearest to 10 possible with these digits is

_____

The number nearest to 100 was

_____

The number nearest to 100 possible with these digits is

_____

1B Place value

Explore

Multiplying by 10, 100 and 1000

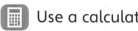 Use a calculator for this activity.

- Put any four-digit number into your calculator.

- Write the number in the place value grid below.

- Multiply the number by 10.

- Write the answer in the place value grid.

- Multiply the number by 100.

- Write the answer in the place value grid.

- Multiply the number by 1000.

- Write the answer in the place value grid.

- Repeat this for two other four-digit numbers.

Millions	Hundred thousands	Ten thousands	Thousands	Hundreds	Tens	Units

- Now complete these phrases:

When you multiply by 10 the digits move _____ places to the _____

When you multiply by 100 _____

When you multiply by 1000 _____

Dividing by 10, 100 and 1000

Use a calculator for this activity.

- Put any three-digit number into your calculator.
- Write the number in the place value grid below.
- Divide the number by 10.
- Write the answer in the place value grid.
- Divide the number by 100.
- Write the answer in the place value grid.
- Divide the number by 1000.
- Write the answer in the place value grid.
- Repeat this for two other three-digit numbers.

Hundreds	Tens	Units	Decimal point	Tenths	Hundredths	Thousandths
			•			
			•			
			•			
			•			
			•			
			•			
			•			
			•			
			•			
			•			
			•			
			•			

- Now complete these phrases:

When you divide by 10 the digits move _____ places to the _____

When you divide by 100 _____

When you divide by 1000 _____

Discover

Prime and composite numbers

A **factor** of a number is a number that divides exactly into that number. For example $6 \div 3 = 2$ so 3 is a factor of 6 and $6 \div 2 = 3$ so 2 is also a factor of 6.

A **prime number** is a number that has only two factors: itself and 1. You can use 'the sieve of Eratosthenes' to find all the prime numbers up to 100. Eratosthenes was an Ancient Greek mathematician.

1	2	3	4	5	6	7	8	9	10
11	12	13	14	15	16	17	18	19	20
21	22	23	24	25	26	27	28	29	30
31	32	33	34	35	36	37	38	39	40
41	42	43	44	45	46	47	48	49	50
51	52	53	54	55	56	57	58	59	60
61	62	63	64	65	66	67	68	69	70
71	72	73	74	75	76	77	78	79	80
81	82	83	84	85	86	87	88	89	90
91	92	93	94	95	96	97	98	99	100

- Use this 100 square to make a sieve of Eratosthenes:

  - 1 is not a prime number. It only has one factor. Circle the number 1.

  - The number 2 is a prime number. Shade the number 2.

  - The number 2 is a factor of the multiples of 2. The multiples of 2 are not prime numbers. Cross out all the multiples of 2.

  - The number 3 is a prime number. Shade the number 3.

  - The number 3 is a factor of the multiples of 3. The multiples of 3 are not prime numbers. Cross out all the multiples of 3.

- The number 5 is a prime number. Shade the number 5.

- The number 5 is a factor of the multiples of 5. The multiples of 5 are not prime numbers. Cross out all the multiples of 5.

- Repeat with the other prime numbers. Each time start with the next prime number.

- Now list all the prime numbers up to 100:

  Prime numbers: 2, 3, 5, 7, _____

  _____

A **composite number** is a number which has more than 2 factors.

You can divide all composite numbers into **prime factors**.

You can use a factor tree to find the prime factors of any number.

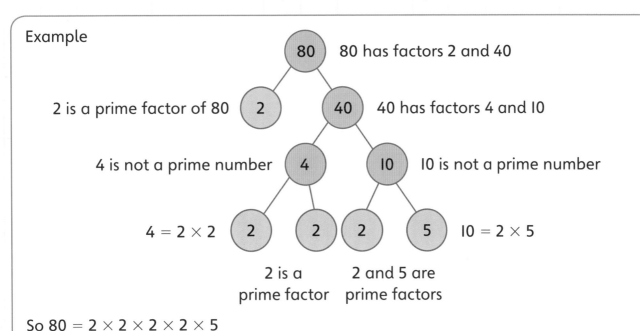

Example

80 has factors 2 and 40

2 is a prime factor of 80

40 has factors 4 and 10

4 is not a prime number

10 is not a prime number

4 = 2 × 2

10 = 2 × 5

2 is a prime factor

2 and 5 are prime factors

So 80 = 2 × 2 × 2 × 2 × 5

2, 2, 2, 2 and 5 are the prime factors of 80.

• Now find the prime factors of these numbers:

150   36   75

1C Number properties

Explore

Finding factors of two-digit numbers

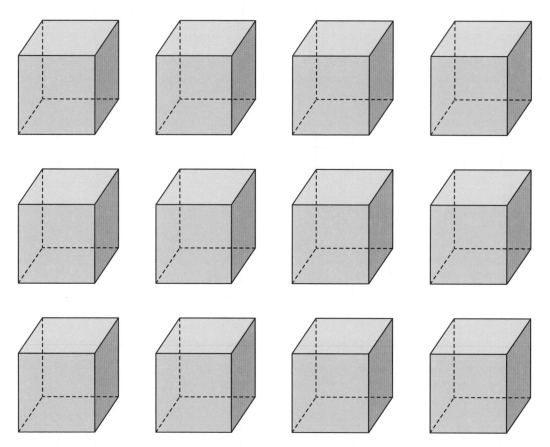

This shows that you can write 12 as 3 × 4.

We say that 4 and 3 are factors of 12. They divide exactly into 12.

How many ways can you arrange 12 cubes?

• Find all the different ways. Then complete this sentence:

The factors of 12 are _____

Repeat this for 18, 24, 36 and 49 cubes.

• Write the factors:

The factors of 18 are _____

The factors of 24 are _____

The factors of 36 are _____

The factors of 49 are _____

Common multiples

- Complete this Venn diagram:

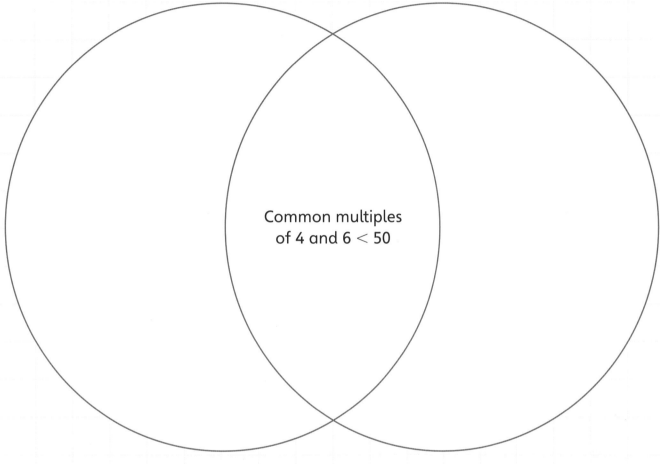

Common multiples
of 4 and 6 < 50

Multiples of 4 < 50   Multiples of 6 < 50

The numbers in both multiplication tables are the **common multiples** of 4 and 6.

- Write the common multiples less than 50 of these numbers:

3 and 7 _____

_____

2 and 10 _____

_____

5 and 12 _____

_____

6 and 9 _____

_____

2, 3 and 5 _____

_____

1D Comparing numbers

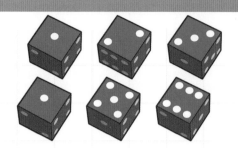

Discover

From the numbers on these dice, I can make 161235 and 523611.

Roll a dice 6 times and record the numbers below.

Make 10 different six-digit numbers and write them here

_____   _____   _____

_____   _____   _____

Now order your numbers from smallest to largest.

Smallest	
Largest	

Roll the dice again: roll it 10 times to make 5 two-digit negative numbers. As you roll the dice, list the negative numbers below.

– _____   – _____   – _____   – _____   – _____

Now order these negative numbers from smallest to largest by placing them on the number line.

-20

Smaller

0

Larger

1D Comparing numbers

Explore

Write down these countries in order of population size, starting with the smallest.
Write the size of the population in words next to the country.

Guyana 784 894   Malta 416 055   Djibouti 873 000   Western Sahara 567 000

Tonga 103 036   Barbados 285 000   Brunei 393 162   Bahrain 1 234 571

Country	Population	Population in words

These are the temperatures at which substances solidify (turn solid). Complete the table starting with the liquid which has the lowest solidifying temperature.

Ammonia –78°C   Mercury –39°C   Alcohol –97°C   Aniline –6°C

Water 0°C   Carbon dioxide –78°C   Glycerin –16°C   Lead 327°C

Element	Solidifying point	Solidifying point in words

Discover

- Use a set of 0–9 digit cards.
- Select four cards.
- Use these four digits to make 15 different four-digit numbers.

- Order the numbers smallest to largest.
- Write the numbers in the table.

For example:

I pick 3, 5, 7, 9.

I make 5379, 9357, 7539, and so on.

Number	Number rounded to nearest 10	Number rounded to nearest 100	Number rounded to nearest 1000
5379	5380	5400	5000
7359	7360	7400	7000
9357	9360	9400	9000

Number	Number rounded to nearest 10	Number rounded to nearest 100	Number rounded to nearest 1000

1E Estimation and rounding

Explore

- Use a set of 0–9 digit cards.
- Select four cards.
- Use these digits to make as many different four-digit numbers as you can.
- Write them here:

My four digits are _____

All the possible numbers are _____

_____

I know I have found all the possibilities because _____

_____

- Round all the numbers to the nearest 10.
- Use your numbers to make correct statements:

<   <

>   >

<   <

>   >

<   <

>   >

Placing numbers on empty number lines

- Use 0–9 digit cards.
- Pick four cards to make a four-digit number.
- Label the ends and the middle of the empty number lines.

- Write the number in the correct place.
- Repeat this for each empty number line.

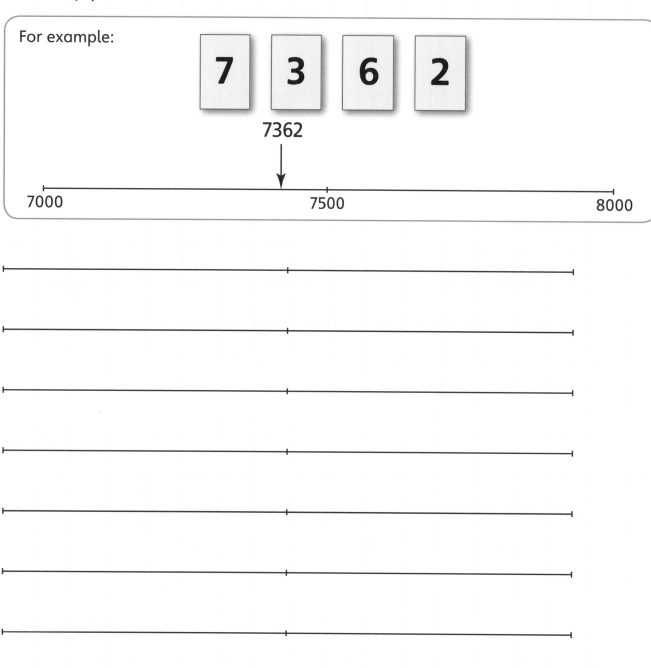

For example:

7 3 6 2

7362

7000   7500   8000

- Use the set of 0–9 digit cards.
- Select 3 cards.
- Make 5 different three-digit numbers with 2 decimal places.

For example if you pick 3, 6 and 8 you could make 3.68, 8.63, 6.38 and so on.

Complete the table below.

Numbers in order of size (smallest first)	Number rounded to nearest tenth

Use these empty number lines to help you. For example,

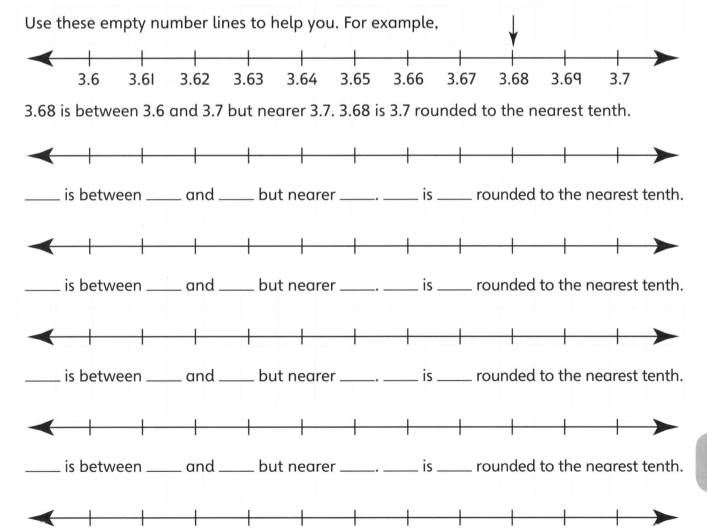

3.68 is between 3.6 and 3.7 but nearer 3.7. 3.68 is 3.7 rounded to the nearest tenth.

_____ is between _____ and _____ but nearer _____. _____ is _____ rounded to the nearest tenth.

_____ is between _____ and _____ but nearer _____. _____ is _____ rounded to the nearest tenth.

_____ is between _____ and _____ but nearer _____. _____ is _____ rounded to the nearest tenth.

_____ is between _____ and _____ but nearer _____. _____ is _____ rounded to the nearest tenth.

_____ is between _____ and _____ but nearer _____. _____ is _____ rounded to the nearest tenth.

1F Number sequences

Discover

This is a famous **sequence**. It is called the Fibonacci sequence.

1, 1, 2, 3, 5, 8, 13, 21,

How do you make the next number in the sequence?

- Write your answers in the spaces.

    The next three numbers in the sequence are _____ _____ _____

    The rule for generating the sequence is _____

    _____

    _____

    A Fibonacci type sequence has 4 and 18 as the first two **terms**. What is the 7th term?

    _____

- Find as many Fibonacci type sequences as you can that contain the term 75.

    > Examples
    >
    > 5, 35, 40, 75   and   23, 26, 49, 75

_____

_____

_____

_____

_____

_____

_____

Here is the start of a sequence:

Position	1	2	3	4	5	6	7
Number	5	9	13	17	21	25	29

The rule for generating the sequence is:

You generate this sequence by adding 4 to the previous number.

- Complete these tables.
- Write the rule for generating the sequence in each table.

Position	1	2	3	4	5	6	7
Number	$\frac{1}{4}$	1	$1\frac{3}{4}$				

You generate this sequence by _____

Position	1	2	3	4	5	6	7
Number	55	25	−5				

You generate this sequence by _____

Position	1	2	3	4	5	6	7
Number	0.8	1.6	2.4				

You generate this sequence by _____

- Make your own sequences in these tables. Give them to a partner to solve.

Position	1	2	3	4	5	6	7
Number							

You generate this sequence by _____

Position	1	2	3	4	5	6	7
Number							

You generate this sequence by _____

1F Number sequences

Odd and even numbers

My number is a three-digit number.

My number is divisible by 5.

My number is a prime number.

- Play 'Crossing the Circle' and 'Making Groups' as a whole class.

- Then complete these sentences:

  The sum of two even numbers is _____

  _____

  The sum of two odd numbers is _____

  _____

  The difference between two even

  numbers is _____

The difference between two odd numbers

is _____

The product of two even numbers is

_____

The product of two odd numbers is

_____

- Write two more general statements about even and odd numbers:

  _____

  _____

1 Number and place value

This is a cuboid made with 48 cubes:

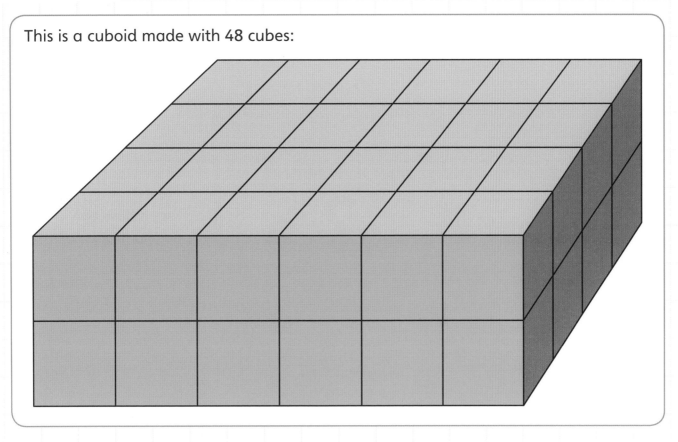

How many different cuboids can you make with 48 cubes?

_____

_____

_____

Choose another starting number to let you make a lot of different cuboids.
Why did you choose this number?

_____

_____

_____

Which starting numbers will only let you make a single cuboid?

_____

_____

_____

1 Number and place value

Guess my number

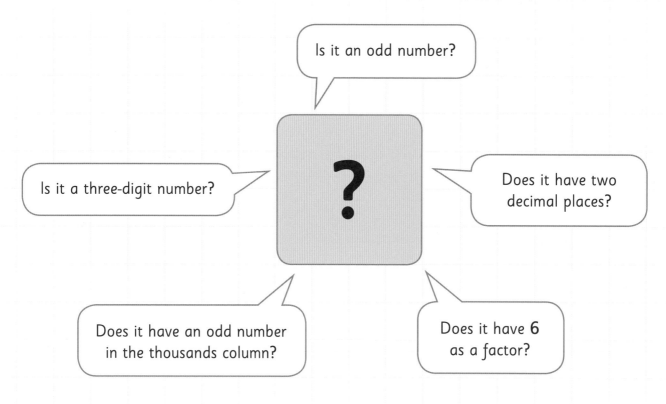

- Pick a two-digit number.
- Write your number in the box.
- Write ten facts about the number.

- Pick any three-digit number.
- Write your number in the box.
- Write ten facts about the number.

2 Fractions and Decimals

2A Equivalent fractions

Discover

How many ways can I make a **quarter**?

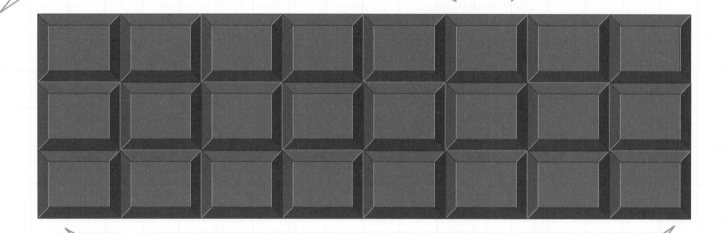

How many different ways can we share this chocolate between four of us?

I think we get six pieces each.

Yes – but there are lots of different ways of doing it.

Do we always get a quarter each?

You could have a row of six pieces or two rows of three pieces.

- Draw three different ways to divide the chocolate bar into quarters.

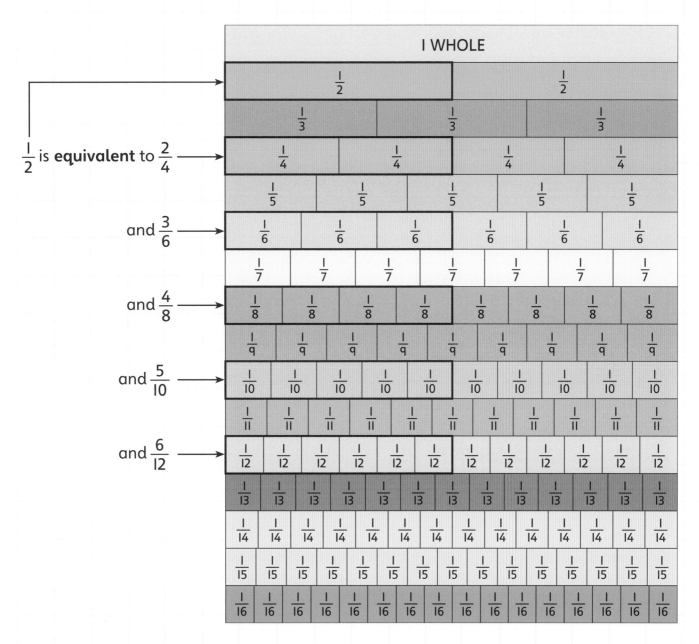

$\frac{1}{2}$ is **equivalent** to $\frac{2}{4}$

and $\frac{3}{6}$

and $\frac{4}{8}$

and $\frac{5}{10}$

and $\frac{6}{12}$

- Use the fraction wall to write five **equivalent fractions** for these:

$\frac{1}{3}$ is equivalent to _____

$\frac{1}{4}$ is equivalent to _____

$\frac{1}{5}$ is equivalent to _____

- Complete these sentences:

Fractions are equivalent to each other if

_____

_____

You can find an equivalent fraction by

_____

2A Equivalent fractions

Explore

I. Complete the grid. Choose your own fractions for the last three rows.

Fraction in its simplest form	Fraction in words	Equivalent fraction	Equivalent fraction	Diagram
$\frac{3}{5}$	Three-fifths	$\frac{6}{10}$	$\frac{9}{15}$	
			$\frac{50}{100}$	
	Four-fifths			
	One-quarter			
$\frac{3}{4}$		$\frac{9}{12}$		
			$\frac{4}{12}$	

The fraction $\frac{3}{5}$ is equivalent to $\frac{6}{10}$.

$\frac{3}{5}$ is in its **simplest form**.

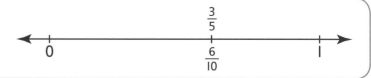

2. Find pairs of equivalent fractions in this list:

$$\frac{1}{4}, \frac{3}{12}, \frac{4}{10}, \frac{9}{12}, \frac{5}{6}, \frac{2}{5}, \frac{1}{2}, \frac{3}{4}, \frac{10}{12}, \frac{6}{12}$$

- For each pair mark the correct position on the number line.
- Write the fraction in its simplest form above the number line.
- Write the equivalent fraction below the number line.

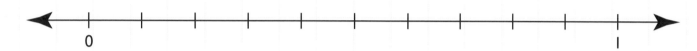

0   1

$$\frac{1}{2}, \frac{3}{8}, \frac{5}{6}, \frac{1}{4}, \frac{7}{8}, \frac{3}{4}$$

To order this set of fractions, use equivalent fractions.

For example: $\frac{3}{4} = \frac{6}{8}$ so $\frac{3}{4} < \frac{7}{8}$

The correct order, starting with the smallest, is:

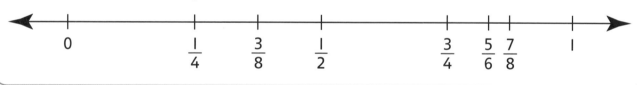

0            $\frac{1}{4}$ $\frac{3}{8}$ $\frac{1}{2}$ $\frac{3}{4}$ $\frac{5}{6}\frac{7}{8}$ 1

3. Order these sets of fractions. Start with the smallest.

$$\frac{3}{4}, \frac{10}{12}, \frac{5}{12}, \frac{1}{2}, \frac{1}{4}, \frac{2}{3}$$

0   1

$$\frac{4}{5}, \frac{3}{10}, \frac{1}{2}, \frac{9}{10}, \frac{2}{5}$$

0   1

2B Fractions and decimals

Discover

- Complete the tables below by changing the **fractions** to **decimals**. Then write a sentence about what you notice.

Fraction	$\frac{1}{4}$	$\frac{2}{4}$	$\frac{3}{4}$	$\frac{4}{4}$	$\frac{5}{4}$
Decimal equivalent					

Fraction	$\frac{1}{5}$	$\frac{2}{5}$	$\frac{3}{5}$	$\frac{4}{5}$	$\frac{5}{5}$
Decimal equivalent					

Fraction	$\frac{1}{8}$	$\frac{2}{8}$	$\frac{3}{8}$	$\frac{4}{8}$	$\frac{5}{8}$	$\frac{6}{8}$	$\frac{7}{8}$	$\frac{8}{8}$
Decimal equivalent								

Fraction	$\frac{1}{12}$	$\frac{2}{12}$	$\frac{3}{12}$	$\frac{4}{12}$	$\frac{5}{12}$	$\frac{6}{12}$	$\frac{7}{12}$	$\frac{8}{12}$	$\frac{9}{12}$	$\frac{10}{12}$	$\frac{11}{12}$	$\frac{12}{12}$
Decimal equivalent												

I notice that _____

_____

- Try this with other families of fractions and their decimal equivalents.

2B Fractions and decimals

Explore

I. Write five fractions between 0 and I in the table.

- Write down their decimal equivalents.

Fraction						
Decimal equivalent						

2. Complete this table to show fractions and their decimal equivalents:

0.3	$\frac{3}{10}$	three-tenths
0.30	$\frac{30}{100}$	_____-hundredths
0.300		_____-thousandths
0.7		_____-tenths
0.70	$\frac{70}{100}$	
	$\frac{700}{1000}$	
	$\frac{9}{10}$	
		ninety-hundredths
0.900		

What do you notice about these fractions and their decimal equivalents?

_____

_____

_____

3. Here are the results for the Men's 100 m final in the Olympics in 2012.

- In the blank table, write the results in order. Start with the fastest time.

Athlete	Time (seconds)
Ryan Bailey	9.88
Yohan Blake	9.75
Usain Bolt	9.63
Justin Gatlin	9.79
Tyson Gay	9.80
Churandy Muranda	9.94
Asafa Powell	11.99
Richard Thompson	9.98

Athlete	Time (seconds)

4. Here are the results for the women's high jump final.

- In the blank table below, write the results in order. Start with the highest jump.

Athlete	Height of jump (metres)
Burcu Ayhan	1.87
Brigetta Barrett	2.03
Ruth Beita	1.89
Anna Chicherova	2.05
Irina Gordeeva	1.93
Emma Green	1.95
Tia Hellebaut	1.99
Chaunte Lowe	1.97
Melanie Melfort	1.91
Airine Palsyte	1.90
Svetlana Radzivil	1.94
Svetlana Shkolina	2.02

Athlete	Height of jump (metres)

2C Addition pairs

I know that 78 + 22 = 100 so that means 7.8 + 2.2 = 10 and 0.78 + 0.22 = 1

- Use a set of 0–9 digit cards.
- Pick 2 cards.
- Make a two-digit number. Use this number to make addition pairs to 100, 10 and 1.
- Reverse the digits. Use this new number to make addition pairs to 100, 10 and 1.
- Repeat 5 times to complete the table below.

For example, I pick 5 and 6 so

$56 + 44 = 100$; $5.6 + 4.4 = 10$ and $0.56 + 0.44 = 1$, and

$65 + 45 = 100$; $6.5 + 4.5 = 100$ and $0.65 + 0.45 = 1$

Number	Addition pair to 100	Addition pair to 10	Addition pair to 1

2C Addition pairs

Use your knowledge of addition pairs to complete these diagrams:

I.

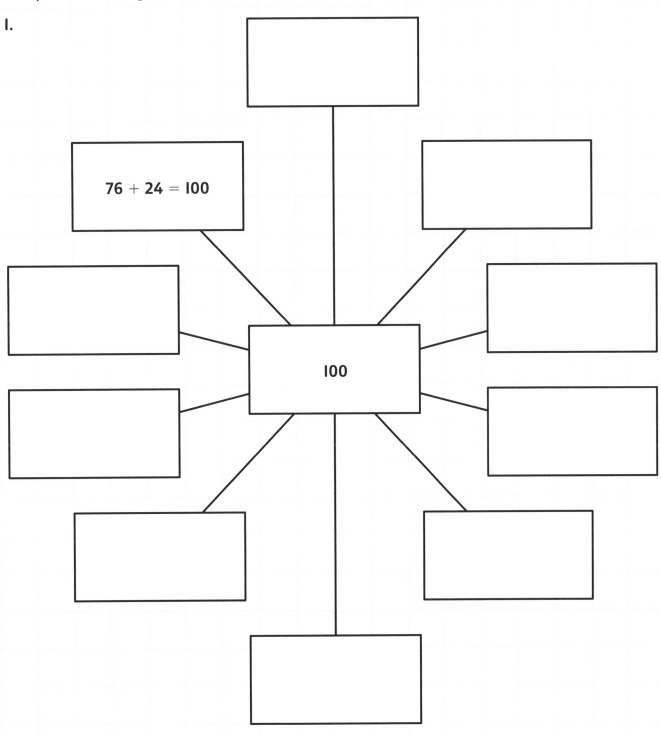

2.

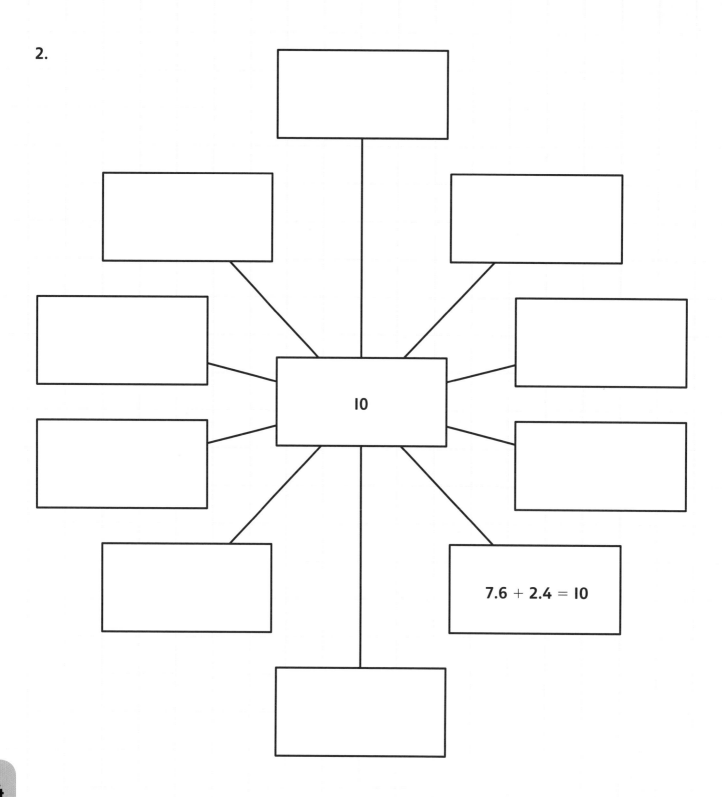

10

7.6 + 2.4 = 10

3.

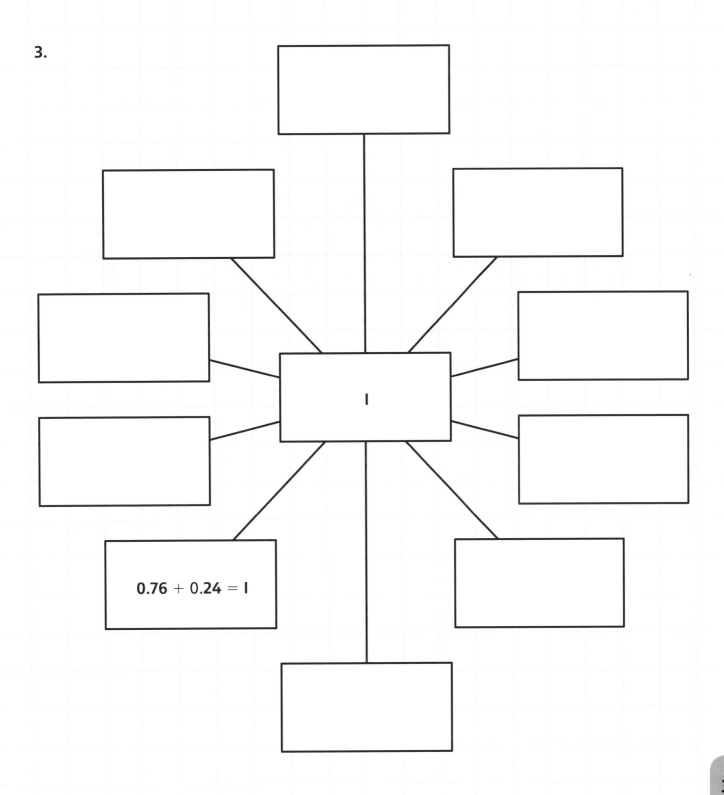

$$0.76 + 0.24 = 1$$

2D Mixed numbers and improper fractions

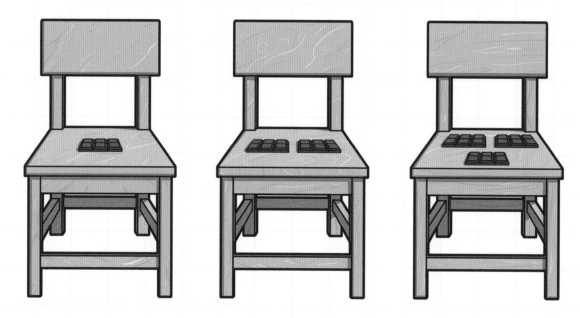

There are ten students in your class. They come into the classroom one at a time and stand behind one of the three chairs. They cannot change their position. Students behind each chair share the chocolate on that chair.

Where should they stand to share out the chocolate as fairly as possible?

• Draw or write your solution here:

2D Mixed numbers and fractions

Explore

1. a) You have **three** pizzas to share with a friend. How much pizza do you **get each**?

    _____

    b) **Two** more friends arrive. How much pizza do you **get each** now?

    _____

2. a) The next day your dad buys five small cakes. He divides the cakes into thirds. You take it in turns to eat some cake. The table below shows how much cake everyone eats. Complete the table to see how much is left for you.

	Number of cakes eaten	Number of cakes left
	None	5
Dad	$1\frac{1}{3}$	$3\frac{2}{3}$
Mum	$\frac{2}{3}$	
Big brother	$1\frac{2}{3}$	
Big sister	$\frac{2}{3}$	
You		

b) Write your own story and complete the table below:

_____

_____

_____

_____

	Amount of cake eaten	Amount of cake left
	None	
Dad		
Mum		
Big brother		
Big sister		
You		

3. a) **Three** people are eating chapatis. They eat $\frac{3}{4}$ of a chapati each.

    How many chapatis do they eat in total?

    _____

    b) **Five** people are eating pizza. They eat $\frac{1}{2}$ of a pizza each.

    How many pizzas do they eat in total?

    _____

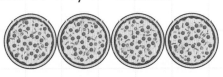

c) Two people are eating small cakes.
    They eat $1\frac{1}{2}$ each.

How many cakes do they eat in total?

_____

d) Seven people are eating cookies.
    They eat $\frac{1}{3}$ of a cookie each.

How many cookies do they eat in total?

_____

4. Draw a picture to show each of these fractions:

A fraction between $1\frac{1}{2}$ and 3	A fraction smaller than 5
A fraction larger than $\frac{3}{4}$	A fraction smaller than $1\frac{3}{4}$

5. | $\frac{3}{4}$ is equivalent to $\frac{12}{16}$.

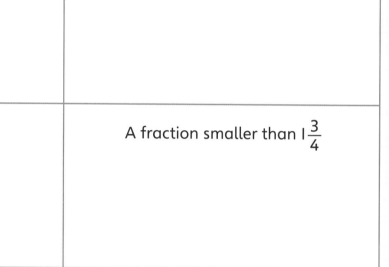

• Find pairs of equivalent fractions in this list.

• Write one fraction from each pair above the line in its correct place.

• Write the other fraction below the line in its correct place.

$\frac{10}{16}$, $\frac{5}{8}$, $\frac{7}{6}$, $1\frac{2}{3}$, $\frac{20}{12}$, $1\frac{1}{2}$, $1\frac{1}{6}$, $\frac{15}{10}$

38

2E Ratio and proportion

I. You can buy green paint from two companies.

Paint A is made up from blue and yellow paint in the ratio I : 4.

Paint B is made up from blue and yellow paint in the ratio I : 7.

You can mix blue and yellow to make different shades of green.

Paint A and Paint B are in the same size tins.

Paint A   Paint B

You are making different shades of green. You don't want to use too much paint!

How many tins of paints A and B do you need to make green paint with these ratios of blue to yellow?

I : 5 _____

I : 6 _____

2. You want to paint another room orange.

Orange paint is made up from yellow and red paint.

Paint C   Paint D

Paint C is made up from red and yellow in the ratio I : 4.

Paint D is made up from red and yellow in the ratio I : 9.

What is the minimum number of tins of paints C and D you need to make orange made up from red and yellow in the following ratios?

I : 5 _____

I : 6 _____

I : 7 _____

I : 8 _____

3. Make up a similar question for your partner to solve:

You want to paint another room

_____.

_____ paint is made up from

_____ and _____ paint.

Paint E is made up from _____

and _____ in the ratio ___ : ___.

Paint F is made up from _____

and _____ in the ratio ___ : ___.

What is the minimum number of tins of paints E and F you need to make

_____ made up from _____

and _____ in the following ratios?

___ : ___ _____

___ : ___ _____

___ : ___ _____

2E Ratio and proportion

Explore

1. I use this paint to paint my bedroom walls.

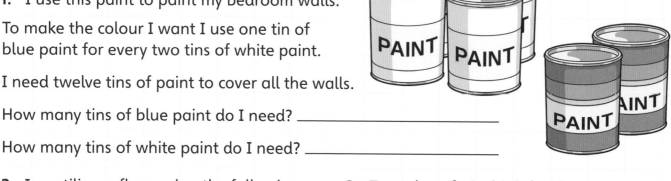

To make the colour I want I use one tin of blue paint for every two tins of white paint.

I need twelve tins of paint to cover all the walls.

How many tins of blue paint do I need? _____

How many tins of white paint do I need? _____

2. I am tiling a floor using the following pattern of tiles:

The pattern uses one black tile for every two white tiles.

My room is six tiles wide and twelve tiles long.

a) How many black tiles do I need?

_____

b) How many white tiles do I need?

_____

c) I buy 39 tiles in the correct ratio. How many white tiles do I buy?

_____

3. To make a fruit drink for three people, I mix fruit juice and water in the ratio 1 part fruit juice to 3 parts water. This makes 200 millilitres of fruit drink.

a) How much fruit juice do I need for six people?

_____

b) How much water do I use for 150 millilitres of fruit juice?

_____

2F Percentages

Discover

1. Here are three circles.

   - Shade in 25% of the first circle.
   - Shade in 50% of the second circle.
   - Shade in 75% of the third circle.

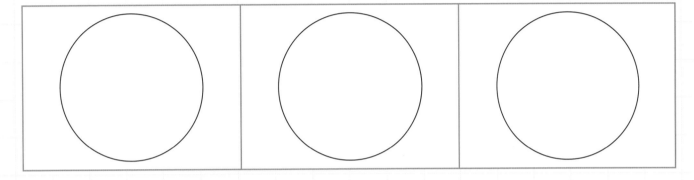

2. The total number of marks in a test is 80.

   The table shows some possible marks out of 80.

   - Complete the table to show the equivalent percentage scores:

Marks	Percentage
80	100%
70	
60	
55	
45	
40	
20	
10	
8	10%
4	
2	
1	
0	0%

2F Percentages

• Complete this table:

Fraction	Decimal fraction	Percentage	Percentage as an area
$\frac{1}{10}$	0.1	10%	
$\frac{1}{5}$			
$\frac{1}{4}$			
$\frac{3}{10}$			
$\frac{2}{5}$			
$\frac{1}{2}$			
$\frac{3}{5}$			
$\frac{7}{10}$			
$\frac{3}{4}$			
$\frac{4}{5}$			
1 whole			

2 Fractions and decimals

Connect

You are a shopkeeper. You sell the following items:

Item	Usual selling price	Cost price
T-shirt	6 dollars	2 dollars
Shorts	8 dollars	3 dollars
Jeans	14 dollars	10 dollars
Sandals	5 dollars	2 dollars

You reduce the price of these items in a sale. You reduce:

one item by 10%

one item by 15%

one item by a quarter

one item by a half.

Last year you sold these items in the following proportions:

Item	Percentage sales
T-shirts	40
Shorts	30
Jeans	20
Sandals	10

Which items do you reduce by which percentage?

- Write a presentation to explain your decision to your class:

I reduce _____ by _____ %

because _____

I reduce _____ by _____ %

because _____

I reduce _____ by _____ %

because _____

I reduce _____ by _____ %

because _____

2 Fractions and decimals

- Write or draw fractions or percentages in the empty squares.
- Cut the cards out.
- Use the cards to play the memory game with your partner.

0.8	$\frac{1}{2}$	60%	
	75%		$\frac{7}{10}$
50%	$\frac{4}{5}$	0.75	
	80%		0.7
$\frac{3}{5}$		0.5	
$\frac{3}{4}$		70%	

3 Mental Calculation

3A Mental strategies for addition and subtraction

Discover

1. I am thinking of two whole numbers that add up to 20.

   What could they be?

   Can you explain your strategy?

2. I am thinking of two numbers.

   Each number has **one decimal place**.

   The two numbers add up to 2.

   What could they be?

3. I am thinking of two numbers.

   Each number has one decimal place.

   The two numbers add up to 1.

   What could they be?

   To work out a pair of numbers with **two decimal places** that add up to 1:

   I _____

   _____

   I know that this is correct because

   _____

   _____

4. I am thinking of two numbers.

   Each number has two decimal places.

   The two numbers add up to 1.

   Write down ten possibilities for the two numbers.

Adding two-digit and three-digit numbers

5. This table gives the numbers of students in each class in a school.

   Find two different ways to work out the total number of students in the school.

Class	Number of students
Kindergarten	42
Grade 1	28
Grade 2	35
Grade 3	33
Grade 4	35
Grade 5	33
Grade 6	27

6. This table shows how many people got on and off a bus at each stop.

Stop	Number getting on bus	Number getting off bus
Bus Station	38	0
Cinema	9	5
School	15	3
Temple	11	12
Shopping Mall	26	14
Riverside	7	9
Sports Stadium	3	24

Read the information out to your partner.

Ask your partner to write down how many people are on the bus when it leaves the Sports Stadium.

Ask your partner to tell you their answer.

Did you get the same answer?

3A Mental strategies for addition and subtraction

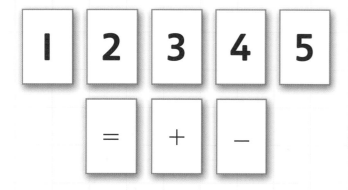

Use the digits 1, 2, 3, 4 and 5 once and only once.

- Make a **sum** with two numbers.
  For example: 123 + 45 = 168

- Make a sum with three numbers.
  For example: 12 + 34 + 5 = 51

- Make a subtraction with two numbers.
  For example: 312 − 54 = 258

1. Use the digits 1, 2, 3, 4 and 5 once and only once. Find:

   a) the largest sum with two numbers

   _____

   b) the largest sum with three numbers

   _____

   c) the smallest sum with two numbers

   _____

   d) the smallest sum with three
      numbers _____

   e) the largest difference between two
      numbers _____

   f) the smallest difference between
      two numbers _____

g) the largest answer you can get
   using all the cards _____

h) the smallest answer you can get
   using all the cards _____

2. The answer is 112.
   What is the calculation?

   Write down ten different calculations involving **two-digit and three-digit numbers** and **addition** and **subtraction**:

   a) _____ = 112

   b) _____ = 112

   c) _____ = 112

   d) _____ = 112

   e) _____ = 112

   f) _____ = 112

   g) _____ = 112

   h) _____ = 112

   i) _____ = 112

   j) _____ = 112

3. Can you find a quick way to add together all the numbers from 1 to 100?

3B Mental strategies for multiplication and division

Discover

I. Here is 36 as an **array**:

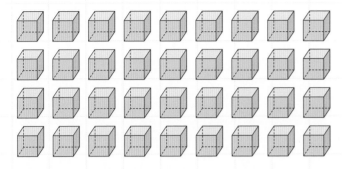

How many different ways can you draw
36 as an array?

- Sketch them here:

2. Repeat question I for the numbers 24,
    28, 32 and 40:

3. Complete these calculations:

$15 \times 9 =$	$15 \times 11 =$
$16 \times 9 =$	$16 \times 11 =$
$17 \times 9 =$	$17 \times 11 =$
$18 \times 9 =$	$18 \times 11 =$
$19 \times 9 =$	$19 \times 11 =$
$20 \times 9 =$	$20 \times 11 =$
$21 \times 9 =$	$21 \times 11 =$

What do you notice about the answers? Complete these sentences:

a) A quick way to multiply any number by 9 is to _____ and then _____

b) A quick way to multiply any number by 11 is to _____ and then _____

4. Work in groups to find rules for **divisibility** for each of the times tables.
   Then write down the rules in this table.

Multiplication table	Rule
A number divides by 2 if	
A number divides by 3 if	
A number divides by 4 if	
A number divides by 5 if	
A number divides by 6 if	
A number divides by 7 if	
A number divides by 8 if	
A number divides by 9 if	
A number divides by 10 if	

3B Mental strategies for multiplication and division

- Complete these tables
- First do the calculations in your head.
- Then check your results with a calculator.
- Then complete the sentences.

I. Multiplying pairs of **multiples of 10**

×	10	30	50	60	90
10					
20					
30					
40					
70					

To multiply multiples of ten I _____

_____

2. Multiplying **near multiples of 10**

×	10	30	50	60
19				
21				
39				
41				
51				
69				
91				

To multiply near multiples of ten I

_____

3. Multiplying by **numbers with one decimal place**

×	18	25	40	80
0.2				
0.4				
0.8				
0.6				
0.5				
0.9				
0.7				

To multiply by numbers with one decimal place I _____

_____

_____

3C Using known facts to derive new ones

Discover

1. Complete this multiplication table:

×	0.25	0.5	2	5	10	20	50	70	90	100
3										
6										
9										
10										
30										
60										
70										

- Talk to a partner about how you completed the table:

First I _____ and then I _____

2. Make a multiplication table for your partner to complete.

- Use numbers that link to help your partner complete the table:

×										

3. Use the 17 times table to complete the following table:

17 times table	Reason
1 × 17 =	
2 × 17 =	
3 × 17 = 51	3 × 10 = 30 and 3 × 7 = 21 and 30 + 21 = 51
4 × 17 =	
5 × 17 =	
6 × 17 =	
7 × 17 =	
8 × 17 =	
9 × 17 =	
10 × 17 —	

Explore

I.

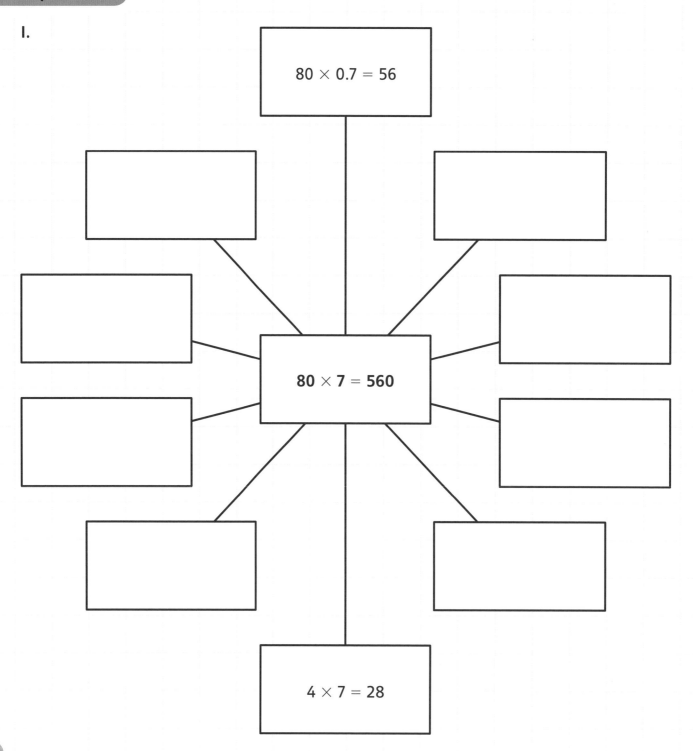

2.

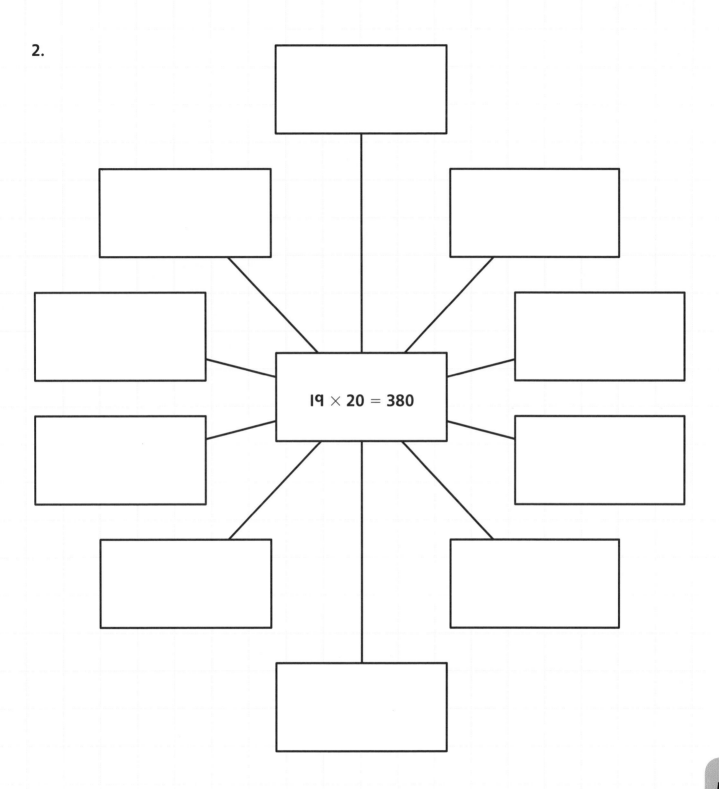

The center box contains: $19 \times 20 = 380$

3D Doubling and halving

Discover

1. Roll a dice twice to make a two-digit number.

   - Write the number in the table.
   - Then **double** the number and write the answer in the table.

   Was it 'easy' or 'hard'? Tick the column and explain why.

   Two examples are shown.

Digits	Number	Double	Easy	Hard	Reason
2, 1	21	42	✓		This is easy because I double **20** then add **2**.
5, 6	56	112		✓	Because it goes over **100**. I double **50** and double **6**, then add the answers together.

2. Roll a dice three times to make a three-digit number.

   - Write the number in the table.
   - **Halve** the number and write the answer in the table.

   Was it 'easy' or 'hard'? Tick the column and explain why.

   Two examples are shown.

Digits	Number	Half of the number	Easy	Hard	Reason
1, 6, 2	162	81	✓		This is easy because half of **160** is **80** and half of **2** is **1**. Then I add them.

5, 5, 6	556	278		✓	Because it is a bigger number. I know that half of **500** is **250**, and half of **50** is **25**, and half of **6** is **3**. Then I add them.

3. Complete this table.

- Explain how you calculated the answers.

Question	Answer	Strategy
Double 2.44		
Double 7.5		
Halve 2.44		
Double 3.2		
Halve 3.2		
Halve 6.88		
Double 14.8		
Halve 25.6		
Halve 2.44		
Double 35.9		

3D Doubling and halving

1. These are the prices of clothes in a shop:

Shorts 18 dollars   T-shirt 15 dollars   Sandals 24 dollars

a) You buy two T-shirts and two pairs of shorts. How much does this cost?

b) Your friend buys one pair of sandals and four T-shirts. What do they spend?

c) All items are half price in a sale. What is the total cost of one pair of shorts, one T-shirt and one pair of sandals?

d) Write two more questions for your friends. Include doubling or halving.

2.

- Complete the prices on these shopping lists:

a)
SHOPPING LIST
200 g Banana
50 g Mango
400 g Pomegranate

b)
SHOPPING LIST
50 g Banana
200 g Mango
200 g Pomegranate

c)
SHOPPING LIST
150 g Banana
300 g Mango
150 g Pomegranate

d)
SHOPPING LIST
300 g Banana
200 g Mango
300 g Pomegranate

3. Use the Fish Stew recipe to write two questions that you can solve mentally.

- Include doubling and halving in your questions.
- Make your questions as hard as you can.
- Ask your friends your questions.

Fish Stew (Serves 4)

300 g fish
2 cloves of garlic
1 teaspoon cumin
200 g tomatoes
1 pepper
$\frac{1}{2}$ lemon

3E Mental strategies for division of two-digit numbers by single-digit numbers

Discover

- Use these numbers to make up calculations.

| 1 | 3 | 4 | 6 | 9 | ÷ |

In each calculation, divide a **two-digit number** by a **single-digit number**.

Use a ÷ sign. You can use each digit more than once.

> For example: Division by 3 with a **remainder**: 41 ÷ 3 = 13 r 2
>
> Division by 3 with no remainder: 96 ÷ 3 = 32

- Complete the table:

	Calculation	Answer	Reason
Division by 4 with no remainder			
Division by 4 with a remainder			
Division by 1 with no remainder			
Division by 6 with a remainder			
Division by 9 with a remainder			
Division by 6 with no remainder			
Division by 3 with a remainder			
Division by 3 with no remainder			
Division by 9 with no remainder			

3E Mental strategies for division of two-digit numbers by single-digit numbers

Explore

- Write a 'revision guide' page to explain the strategies for dividing a two-digit number by a single-digit number.
- Include examples with a remainder and without a remainder and an example with a decimal point.

How to divide two-digit numbers by single-digit numbers

3F Adding and subtracting near multiples

Discover

I know that 36 + 9 = 45. If I add 10 to 36 I get 46, so I just need to subtract 1.

I know that 5625 - 999 = 4626. I take 1000 away and then add 1.

Complete the calculations in this table. Explain your method.

Calculation	Explanation
54 + 19 =	
4.3 + 2.9 =	
107 − 98 =	
1998 + 4117 =	
17.5 − 3.1 =	
6743 − 2997 =	
99 + 25 =	
7.2 + 1.9 =	
266 − 98 =	
4123 + 999 =	
27.4 − 4.9 =	
105 − 15 =	
69 + 19 =	
852 − 303 =	

3F Adding and subtracting near multiples

Ali's Store
Magazine prices
Sports magazines: $3.99
Travel magazines: $2.97
Puzzle magazines: $1.98
Fashion magazines: $4.98

Make up 6 questions for your partners to solve. There should be 3 addition problems and 3 subtraction problems.

3 Mental calculation

1. Complete this **addition** grid with your digits.

   - Roll a dice nine times and fill the cells one at a time.

   - Then **add** the three numbers.

   For example: 24 . 6
                31 . 2
                54 . 1
              ‾‾‾‾‾‾‾
             109 . 9

   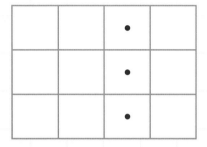

   Play with your friends. The winner is the person with the answer nearest to 100.

2. Complete this **subtraction** grid.

   Roll a dice and fill the cells one at a time.

   For example: 26.5 − 15.2 = 11.3

   Play with your friends. The winner is the person with the answer nearest to 10.

3. Complete this **multiplication** grid.

   Roll a dice and fill the cells one at a time.

   For example: 262 × 4 = 1048

   Play with your friends. The winner is the person with the answer nearest to 1000.

4. Complete this **division** grid.

   Roll a dice and fill the cells one at a time.

   For example: 66.2 ÷ 5 = 13.24

   Play with your friends. The winner is the person with the answer nearest to 10.

3 Mental calculation

- Make a set of loop cards like the ones below to play with your friends.
  You can take them home and play with your family.

I am 0.5 Who is 29 + 13?	I am 42 Who is 98 − 23?	I am 75 Who is 6 × 14?	I am 84 Who is 120 ÷ 6
I am 20 Who is 19 + 57?	I am 76 Who is 136 − 23?	I am 113 Who is 9 × 18?	I am 162 Who is 100 ÷ 4?
I am 25 Who is 2.8 + 17?	I am 19.8 Who is 5.5 − 2.3?	I am 3.2 Who is 0.5 × 7?	I am 3.5 Who is 180 ÷ 4?
I am 45 Who is 115 + 76?	I am 191 Who is 89 − 6?	I am 83 Who is 10 × 2.7?	I am 27 Who is 66 ÷ 3?
I am 22 Who is 1.56 + 2.33?	I am 3.89 Who is 15.5 − 10.5?	I am 5 Who is 100 × 1.37?	I am 137 Who is 8 ÷ 16?

4 Addition and Subtraction

Engage

Each letter stands for a digit.
What does each letter represent?

Oh, so 'E' could represent **7**.

One plus six is four –
what does it mean?

$$
\begin{array}{r}
\text{ONE} \\
+\ \text{SIX} \\
\hline
\text{FOUR}
\end{array}
$$

Should we try
some examples?

We can't do
this mentally.

Do you think the
units column adds up
to more than 10?

67

Discover

- Look at each of these calculations.

  Can you work them out mentally or do you need to use a paper and pencil method?

- Explain your answers.

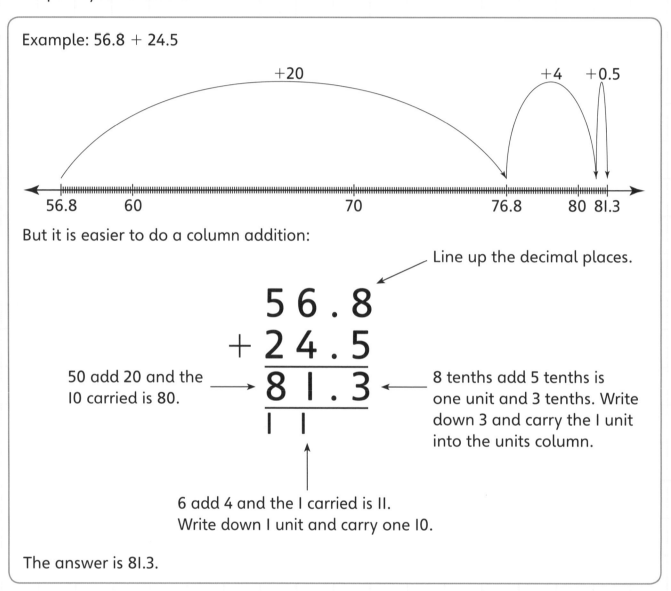

Example: 56.8 + 24.5

But it is easier to do a column addition:

Line up the decimal places.

$$
\begin{array}{r}
5\ 6 . 8 \\
+\ 2\ 4 . 5 \\
\hline
8\ 1 . 3 \\
\hline
1\ \ 1
\end{array}
$$

50 add 20 and the 10 carried is 80.

8 tenths add 5 tenths is one unit and 3 tenths. Write down 3 and carry the 1 unit into the units column.

6 add 4 and the 1 carried is 11.
Write down 1 unit and carry one 10.

The answer is 81.3.

1. 152.7 + 14.1

2. 45 + 17

3. 983.7 + 419.8

4. 115.5 − 16.2

5. 101 − 17

6. 51.52 + 13.11

7. 121.78 + 19.44

8. 452.2 − 134.8

9. 52.12 + 9.57

10. 147.9 + 321.6

4A Adding and subtracting three-digit numbers

- Use the digits 4, 5, 6, 7, 8, 9 to make two three-digit numbers.

1. What is the smallest possible sum?

2. What is the largest possible sum?

3. Create sums with the answer as close as possible to each of the numbers in the table.

> For example: for 900: 576 + 489 = 1065

Can you make a sum closer to 900?

900	1200
1300	1400
1500	1600
1700	1800

4. Check these calculations.
If they are correct, 'tick' them.
If there is an error, explain where the student has made a mistake.

985 − 668 317	27.5 + 42.6 69.11
456 + 845 1291	38.9 + 46.5 85.4
876 − 459 417	76.5 − 32.8 43.7
76.5 − 32.8 44.3	576 + 345 921
346 + 504 840	1007 − 9 9998

4B Adding and subtracting money

Discover

- Use a set of 0–9 digit cards to create 10 different additions and subtractions in the grids below.

- Then work them out.

They are all money calculations.

> For example
> ```
>   5 3 . 7 2
> + 1 4 . 6 8
> ─────────
>   6 8 . 4 0
> ```

$	Tens	Units		Tenths	Hundredths
			•		
+			•		
			•		

$	Tens	Units		Tenths	Hundredths
			•		
+			•		
			•		

$	Tens	Units		Tenths	Hundredths
			•		
+			•		
			•		

$	Tens	Units		Tenths	Hundredths
			•		
−			•		
			•		

$	Tens	Units		Tenths	Hundredths
			•		
+			•		
			•		

$	Tens	Units		Tenths	Hundredths
			•		
−			•		
			•		

$	Tens	Units		Tenths	Hundredths
			•		
+			•		
			•		

$	Tens	Units		Tenths	Hundredths
			•		
−			•		
			•		

$	Tens	Units		Tenths	Hundredths
			•		
+			•		
			•		

$	Tens	Units		Tenths	Hundredths
			•		
−			•		
			•		

Is the method for **adding decimals** the same as the method for **adding whole numbers**?
Explain your answer.

_____

_____

Is the method for **subtracting decimals** the same as the method for **subtracting whole numbers**?
Explain your answer.

_____

_____

Explore

- Read each of these word problems.
- Write down the **operation** you need to do to solve the problem.
- Then solve the problem.

1. You post two parcels. One parcel weighs 3.56 kg.
   The other parcel weighs 4.82 kg.

   a) What is the total weight of the parcels? _____

   b) How much heavier is the heavier parcel than the

   other parcel? _____

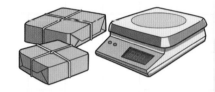

2. The classroom wall is 15.7 m long.
   The whiteboard is 2.2 m long.

   The noticeboard is 3.5 m long.

   How much space is left on the wall?

   _____

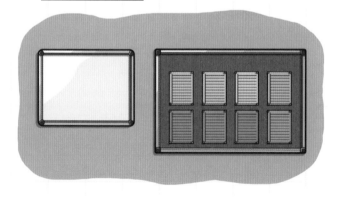

3. You have a 15 gigabyte (GB) Internet
   download allowance per month.
   You use 1.85 GB downloading music
   and 3.65 GB downloading movies.

   How much of your allowance do you

   have left? _____

4. In a 4 × 100 m relay race the four runners' times are 13.46 s, 14.15 s, 12.52 s, 11.99 s.

What is the total time for the race?

_____

5. a) You buy a DVD and a game.

How much do you spend in total?

_____

b) You buy a CD and a DVD.
You pay with a $50 note.

How much change do you receive?

_____

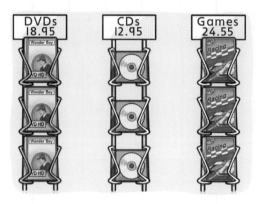

6. Make up two more questions to ask your friends using the prices from question 5.

4C Using negative numbers

Discover

I. a) Match the following temperatures to the thermometers:

London 17°C   Moscow ⁻4°C   Oslo ⁻8°C   Bangkok 35°C   Dubai 42°C

b) Choose six cities around the world.
Use the Internet to find the average temperature for each city in December.
Draw the temperatures on the thermometers below.

Find three positive temperatures and three temperatures below zero.

2. Look at your matched thermometers and cities in question Ia).

a) I fly from Bangkok to London. What is the change in the temperature?

_____

b) Does the temperature rise or fall between Dubai and Bangkok?

_____

By how much? _____

c) Does the temperature rise or fall between London and Moscow?

_____

By how much? _____

d) Does the temperature rise or fall between Moscow and Oslo?

_____

By how much? _____

3. Look at this table of temperatures:

City	Temperature in January
Anchorage	
London	⁻2
Omykan	⁻45
Rio	
Sydney	28
Tunis	
Cairo	
Bangkok	

Use the following clues to complete the table.

- Anchorage is 10 degrees colder than Omykan.
- Rio is 38 degrees warmer than London.
- Tunis is 12 degrees colder than Sydney.
- Cairo is 59 degrees warmer than Omykan.
- Bangkok is 4 degrees colder than Rio.

4C Using negative numbers

- For each of the following statements circle the correct answer.
  The statements are either 'Always true', 'Sometimes true' or 'Never true'.

You add two negative numbers. You get a negative answer. $(^-3) + (^-2)$ Always / sometimes / never	You add a negative number and a positive number. You get a positive answer. $(^-3) + (^+6)$ Always / sometimes / never
You subtract a positive number from a negative number. You get a negative answer. $(^-7) - (^+9)$ Always / sometimes / never	You subtract a negative number from a negative number. You get a negative answer. $(^-4) - (^-6)$ Always / sometimes / never
You subtract a positive number from a positive number. You get a negative answer. $(^+8) - (^+15)$ Always / sometimes / never	You subtract a negative number from a positive number. You get a positive answer. $(^+8) - (^-6)$ Always / sometimes / never

4 Addition and subtraction

Connect

I. The tables show water supply and demand in the Middle East and North Africa.

Supply is how much water is available.

Demand is how much water is needed.

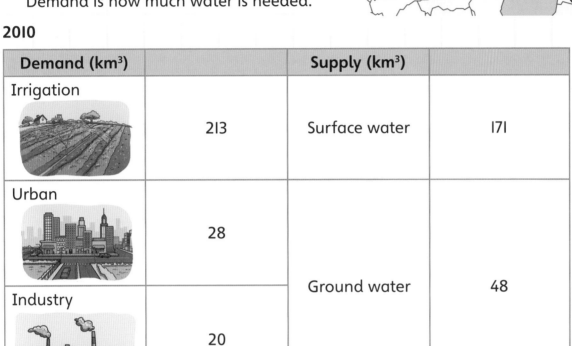

2010

Demand (km³)		Supply (km³)	
Irrigation	213	Surface water	171
Urban	28	Ground water	48
Industry	20		
Total			

2050

Demand (in km³)		Supply (in km³)	
Irrigation	251	Surface water	215
Urban	88	Ground water	168
Industry	41		
Total			

a) Find the totals. Then write them in the tables.

b) What is the difference between supply and demand in 2010? _____

c) What is the predicted difference between supply and demand in 2050? _____

2. Premier League Attendances:

Club		Average attendance	To nearest thousand
Manchester United		75 528	76 000
Arsenal		60 079	
Newcastle United		50 515	
Manchester City		47 017	
Liverpool		44 731	
Chelsea		41 435	
Sunderland		40 601	
Everton		36 182	

Complete the table. Then calculate:

a) the total attendance for these eight clubs _____

b) the difference in attendance between Manchester United
   and Manchester City _____

c) the difference in attendance between Liverpool
   and Everton _____

d) the difference in attendance between Newcastle United
   and Sunderland _____

e) the difference in attendance between the Manchester clubs (United and City)
   and the Liverpool clubs (Liverpool and Everton) _____

4 Addition and subtraction

Review

- Write an example question for each of the following.
- Exchange your questions with a friend.
- Mark your friend's answers and correct any errors.

An addition involving one place of decimals. Write an addition that you solve using a written method.
An addition involving one place of decimals. Write an addition that you solve using a mental method.
A subtraction involving one place of decimals. Write a subtraction that you solve using a written method.
A subtraction involving one place of decimals. Write a subtraction that you solve using a mental method.
An addition involving two places of decimals. Write an addition that you solve using a written method.
An addition involving two places of decimals. Write an addition that you solve using a mental method.
A subtraction involving two places of decimals. Write a subtraction that you solve using a written method.
A subtraction involving two places of decimals. Write a subtraction that you solve using a mental method.

5 Multiplication and Division

There are different ways to work it out.

How can you calculate 286 × 29?

×	20	9	
200	4000	1800	5800
80	1600	720	2320
6	120	54	174
			8294

286 × 29			
	200 × 20	4000	
	80 × 20	1600	
	6 × 20	120	
	200 × 9	1800	
	80 × 9	720	
	6 × 9	54	
		8294	

Which do you think is easiest?

```
    2 8 6
  ×   2 9
  5 7 2 0   (286 × 20)
  2 5 7 4   (286 × 9)
  8 2 9 4
```

Which do you think is quickest?

Discover

I. **Partition** to multiply the following:

a) 346 × 7 = (× 7) + (40 ×   ) + (× 7) = _____

b) $4.92 × 3 = (4 × 3) + (0.9 ×   ) + (× 3) = _____

c) 685 × 6 = (× 6) + (80 ×   ) + (× 6) = _____

d) $4.56 × 4 = (× 4) + (0.5 ×   ) + (× 4) = _____

e) 532 × 8 = _____

f) $8.26 × 5 = _____

2. A friend does not understand this calculation.

- Complete the sentences below to help them:

×	40	7	
300	12000	2100	14100
60	2400	420	2820
5	200	35	235
			17155

This multiplication shows 365 × _____

12 000 in the top left box is the answer to 300 × _____

The first column contains 300, 60 and 5 because _____

2820 is written across from 60 because _____

The answer 17 155 is calculated by _____

Show by estimating that the answer is sensible:

3. Complete these empty boxes to calculate 523 × 47:

×		7	
500	20000		
		140	940
3		21	

Show by estimating that the answer is sensible:

4. Calculate 426 × 82 using the grid below:

×			

Show by estimating that the answer is sensible:

5. Your friend does not understand how to carry out column multiplication. Complete the sentences below to explain it to them:

```
    3 5 2
 ×    6 3
  2 1 1 2 0      (352 × _____ )
    1 0 5 6      (352 × _____ )
  2 2 1 7 6
```

21120 is the answer to _____

1056 is the answer to _____

I get 22176 by _____

6. Write a set of instructions to calculate 415 × 27 using a column method:

You set the multiplication out by _____

_____

First you multiply _____ by _____.

This gives you _____.

Then you multiply _____ by _____.

This gives you _____.

Then you add _____ and _____.

This gives you _____.

You can check the answer by _____

_____.

Explore

| 4 | 5 | 6 | 7 | 8 |

You can use these digits to make a product.

For example:

$45 \times 678 = ?$

$4 \times 5678 = ?$

What is the largest product you can make using the digits **4**, **5**, **6**, **7**, **8**?

- Use each digit only once.
- Use the column method to do the calculations.

5B Dividing three-digit numbers by two-digit numbers

Discover

I. Your friend does not understand how to calculate $845 \div 13$.

Complete the following sentences to explain the method to them:

$$
\begin{array}{r}
65 \\
13\overline{)845} \\
780 \\
\hline
65
\end{array}
$$

$60 \times 13 = 780$

$5 \times 13 = 65$

You write _____ inside the box

and _____ outside _____

because _____.

I tried 60×13 first because _____

_____.

I know $5 \times 13 = 65$ because _____

_____.

The answer is 65 because _____

_____.

You can check the answer by _____

_____.

2. Fill in the blanks to calculate $756 \div 14$:

$$
\begin{array}{r}
\square\square \\
\square\square\overline{)756} \\
700 \\
56
\end{array}
$$

$\square\, 0 \times \square = 700$

$\square \times \square = 56$

Show that the answer is correct using a multiplication:

3. Write a series of instructions to show a friend how to calculate $901 \div 17$:

First you write the division like this _____.

Then you estimate _____.

You write the answer underneath the _____ and _____.

Then you have to _____.

Finally you _____.

You check your answer by _____.

Explore

1. The answer to a division problem is 1331.

    • Use the digits 2, 3, 4 and 5 to find the question.

    • Use a written method to show that you are correct:

2. The answer to a division problem is 52.

    • Use the digits 0, 2, 5 and 6 to find the three-digit **dividend** and the single-digit **divisor**.

    • Use a written method to show that you are correct:

3. The answer to a division question is 15.

    • Use the digits 0, 1, 2, 7 and 8 to find the three-digit dividend and the two-digit divisor.

    • Use a written method to show that you are correct:

4. The answer to a division question is 28.

   - Use the digits 0, 1, 2, 4 and 5 to find the three-digit dividend and the two-digit divisor.

   - Use a written method to show that you are right:

5. Make up a question like question 3 or 4.

   Give your question to a friend to solve.

5C Division with remainders

Discover

1. Write down four different division calculations with an answer including remainder 3.

> For example:
> $45 \div 7 = 6\ r\ 3$
> (Because $7 \times 6 = 42$ so there are 3 left over.)

a) _____

_____

b) _____

_____

c) _____

_____

d) _____

_____

2. Write down four different division calculations with an answer including remainder $\frac{3}{4}$.

> For example:
> $43 \div 4 = 10\frac{3}{4}$
> (Because $4 \times 10 = 40$ and there are 3 left over.
> We are dividing by 4 so that leaves $\frac{3}{4}$.

a) _____

_____

b) _____

_____

c) _____

_____

d) _____

_____

3. Complete the following sentences to explain how to carry out this calculation:

$$\begin{array}{r} 1\ 5\ .\ 6 \\ 5\overline{)7^2 8\ .\ ^3 0} \end{array}$$

This calculation shows how to work out

$78 \div$ _____?

I write 'I' above the '70' because _____

_____.

The next calculation is $28 \div 5$ because

_____.

The answer is 15.6 because _____

_____.

4. Write down two calculations where you multiply a three-digit number with one decimal place by a single-digit number.

Work out your calculations:

5. Write down the division calculation to match each multiplication you wrote in question 4:

5C Division with remainders

Explore

1. Imran wants to get a good deal at the shop.
   - Work out how much each item costs.
   - Circle the better deal for each item.

a

Ice lollies: $6.75 for a box of 10 or $4.47 for a box of 6

b

Cakes: $8.12 for a box of 4 or $12.84 for a box of 6

c

Washing Powder: $18.92 for a 2 kg box or $50.54 for a 7 kg box

d
Juice: $14.35 for a 5-bottle pack or $19.39 for a 7-bottle pack

e
Fizzy Drink: $14.32 for an 8-can pack or $8.25 for a 5-can pack

2. Use the price of the better-value pack to work out the cost of:
   a) 4 ice lollies

Multiplication and Division

b) 7 cakes

c) 3 kg of washing powder

d) 5 bottles of juice

e) 10 fizzy drinks

5D Using the arithmetical laws for multiplication and division

Discover

1. Is each statement 'sometimes true', 'always true' or 'never true'?

   - Circle the correct answer.
   - Give examples to show that you are correct:

I can add numbers in any order and I always get the same answer. sometimes true / always true / never true	I can subtract numbers in any order and I always get the same answer. sometimes true / always true / never true
I can multiply numbers in any order and I always get the same answer. sometimes true / always true / never true	I can divide numbers in any order and I always get the same answer. sometimes true / always true / never true
$a(b + c)$ is always the same as $ab + ac$. sometimes true / always true / never true	$\frac{a + b}{c}$ is always the same as $\frac{a}{c} + \frac{b}{c}$ sometimes true / always true / never true

2. Work in pairs.

- Research the meanings of the following mathematical terms.
- Complete these sentences:

The **associative** law means _____

_____

_____

_____

For example _____

_____

_____

The **commutative** law means _____

_____

_____

_____

For example _____

_____

The **distributive** law means _____

_____

_____

_____

For example _____

_____

_____

5D Using the arithmetical laws for multiplication and division

1. Change the order of the numbers to calculate each answer more easily:

> For example:
> $12 \times 16 \times 5 = 12 \times 5 \times 16 = 60 \times 16 = 960$

a) $20 \times 18 \times 5 =$

b) $15 \times 13 \times 10 =$

c) $18 \times 25 \times 4 =$

d) $5 \times 15 \times 2 =$

e) $4 \times 26 \times 5 =$

2. Use the distributive law to make these calculations easier to work out:

> For example:
> $46 \times 8 = (40 + 6) \times 8 = (40 \times 8) + (6 \times 8) = 320 + 48 = 368$

$27 \times 6 =$

$38 \times 5 =$

$58 \times 7 =$

$62 \times 9 =$

Multiplication and Division

3. Find the missing number in each equation:

$21 + 8 = 40 -$ _____

$22 + 8 = 40 -$ _____

$23 + 8 = 40 -$ _____

$2 \times$ _____ $= 12 + 4$

$2 \times$ _____ $= 12 + 6$

4. Try these number puzzles. Some are correct and some are not correct.

- Change the puzzles that are not correct so that they work.

- Explain how the correct puzzles work.

a) Think of a number.

   Add 3.

   Multiply by 2.

   Subtract 6.

   Divide by 2.

   Your answer is your start number.

   For example, I think of 7:

   $7 + 3 = 10$

   $10 \times 2 = 20$

   $20 - 6 = 14$

   $14 \div 2 = 7$

   So this works for 7.

   Does it work for other numbers?

b) Think of a number.

   Add 3.

   Multiply by 2.

   Subtract 3.

   Divide by 2.

   Your answer is your start number.

c) Think of a number.

   Multiply by 3.

   Add 9.

   Divide by 3.

   Subtract 3.

   Your answer is your start number.

d) Make up a number puzzle like the ones above.

   Give your puzzle to your friends to try.

5 Multiplication and division

Connect

Your class wants to make smoothies to sell to the school.

The food you need to buy is:

One bottle of smoothie uses:

> ### SHOPPING LIST
>
> Mango cost:
> $1.70 per kilogram
>
> Guava cost:
> $1.60 per kilogram
>
> Banana cost:
> $1.20 per kilogram
>
> Yoghurt cost:
> $0.75 a litre

500 g mango

250 g guava

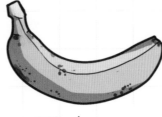

250 g banana

200 ml yoghurt

1. How much does it cost to make 1 bottle of smoothie?

   _____

2. How much does it cost to make 20 bottles of smoothie?

   _____

3. How much does it cost to make 50 bottles of smoothie?

   _____

4. How much does it cost to make 100 bottles of smoothie?

   _____

5. You have $50. How many bottles of smoothie can you make?

   _____

6. You want to make a small profit to buy some new equipment for school.

   a) How much do you sell 1 bottle for?

   _____

   b) You offer a discount for 25 bottles. How much do you sell 25 bottles for?

   _____

5 Multiplication and division

I. Choose two different methods to multiply 3824 by 5.

Under each calculation write an explanation of your method:

2. Choose two different methods to multiply 337 by 23.

Under each calculation write an explanation of your method:

3. Write down three different division questions with an answer ending in 0.6:

4. Write down three different division questions with an answer that has remainder 7:

6 Shapes and Geometry

I can see lots of different shapes.

What is the difference between **2D** and **3D**?

Is a diamond a **regular** shape?

Are those shapes tessellating?

Can a **polygon** have a **curved** line?

Discover

I. Here are some pairs of shapes:

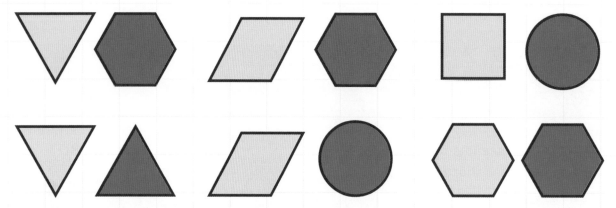

- Copy the shapes onto card and cut them out.
- Use one pair of shapes.
- Move one shape slowly on top of the other shape.
- Stop when the shape is half on top of the other shape.
- What shape is the covered part?
- What shape is the uncovered part?
- Sketch the shapes below and name them:

Repeat for the other pairs of shapes:

2. Repeat the exercise with these pairs of shapes.

What shapes are the uncovered/covered parts?

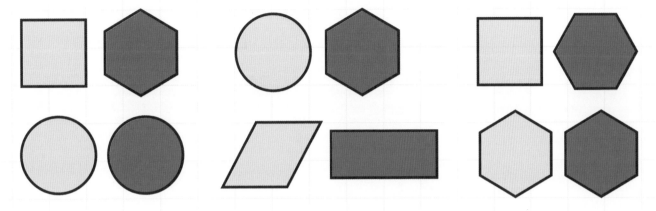

3. Circle and name the overlap shapes that you can find:

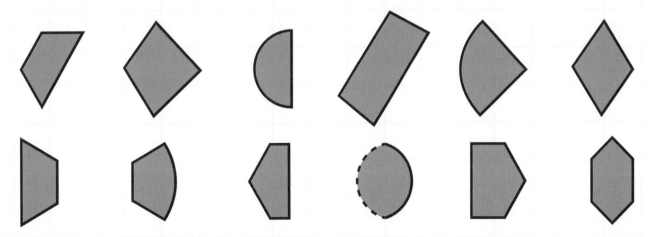

6A Classifying polygons

Explore

1. Draw a different **triangle** in each section of this table and write its name. Are there any sections with no possible triangle? Explain why.

_____

_____

	No right angles	One right angle
No sides equal		
Two sides equal		
Three sides equal		

2. Draw a different **polygon** in each section of this table and write its name:

	Regular	Irregular
Triangle		
Quadrilateral		
Pentagon		
Hexagon		

3. Draw a different polygon in each section of this table and write its name.

	No parallel sides	One pair of parallel sides	Two pairs of parallel sides
No equal sides			
One pair of equal sides			
Two pairs of equal sides			

4. Draw the correct shapes in the second column of this table.

- Write at least three properties for each shape:

Name of shape	Drawing	Properties
Circle		• • •
Equilateral triangle		• • •
Isosceles triangle		• • •
Scalene triangle		• • •

Name of shape	Drawing	Properties
Rectangle		• • •
Square		• • •
Kite		• • •
Parallelogram		• • •
Rhombus		• • •
Regular pentagon		• • •
Irregular hexagon		• • •
Regular octagon		• • •

5. Complete these sentences:

- Draw examples of the shapes.

A shape is a polygon if _____.

These shapes are polygons:

A shape is not a polygon if _____.

These shapes are not polygons:

6B Properties of 3D shapes

Discover

You can use clay and straws to make models of 3D shapes.

For example:

Here is a **cube** and its model:

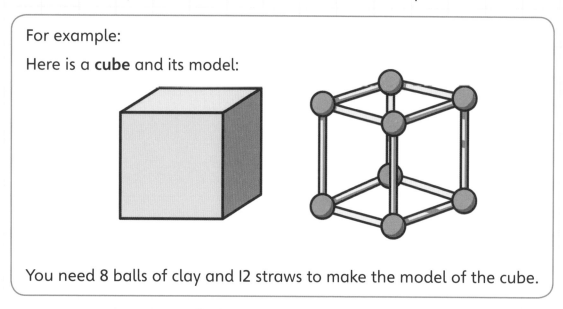

You need 8 balls of clay and 12 straws to make the model of the cube.

- Make models of these shapes:

  How many balls of clay do you need for each shape?

  How many straws do you need?

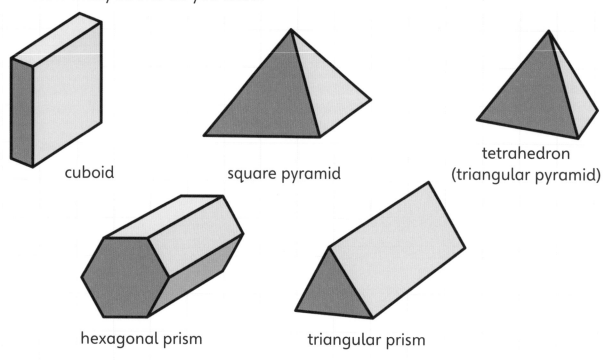

cuboid square pyramid tetrahedron (triangular pyramid)

hexagonal prism triangular prism

- Write your answers in the table.
- Make three models of 3D shapes of your own.
- Add your shapes to the table.

Shape	Number of balls of clay	Number of straws
Cuboid		
Triangular prism		
Square-based pyramid		
Tetrahedron		
Hexagonal prism		

6B Properties of 3D shapes

I. Complete this table to show the properties of each 3D shape:

Can you find an example of each shape in your classroom or the local environment?

	Number of vertices	Number of edges	Number of faces	Example
Cube				
Cuboid				
Pyramid				
Sphere				
Hemisphere				
Cone				
Cylinder				
Prism				
Tetrahedron				
Octahedron				
Dodecahedron				

2. Draw three different cuboids:

3. Draw three different prisms:

4. Draw three different cylinders:

6C Making 2D representations of 3D shapes

Discover

1. This is the **net** of a cube cut into two parts:

    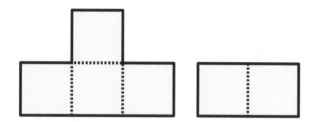

    - Make a copy of the two parts of the net on squared paper.

    - Use the two parts to make the net of a cube.

    - Draw three different ways:

2. Open your interesting-shaped box so that you can see the net.

    - Draw the net:

3. Make a small-scale model of your box so that the length, width and height of the new box are exactly half the size of those of the original box.

    - Sketch this net and write the dimensions:

4. What do you notice about the volume of the new box compared with the original box?

    _____

    _____

    _____

6C Making 2D representations of 3D shapes

You can join four cubes together in lots of different ways.

For example:

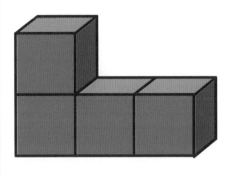

You can draw this arrangement on isometric paper like this:

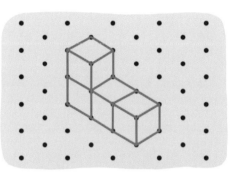

The front elevation is:

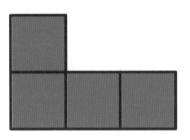

The side elevation is:

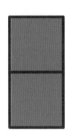

The plan view is:

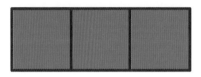

- Use five cubes to make three different models.

- Complete this table:

Plan

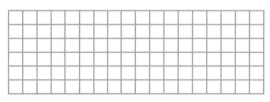

Model I

Front elevation

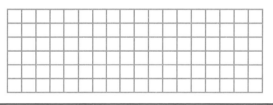

Side elevation

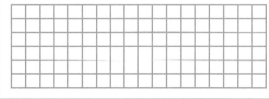

Shapes and Geometry

Model 2

Plan

Front elevation

Side elevation

Model 3

Plan

Front elevation

Side elevation

6D Drawing angles, and angles in a triangle

Discover

- Make triangles on your 9-peg circular pinboards.
- Draw your triangles on the pinboards below.
- Label the acute angles 'a'.
- Label the obtuse angles 'o'.
- Label the reflex angles 'r'.

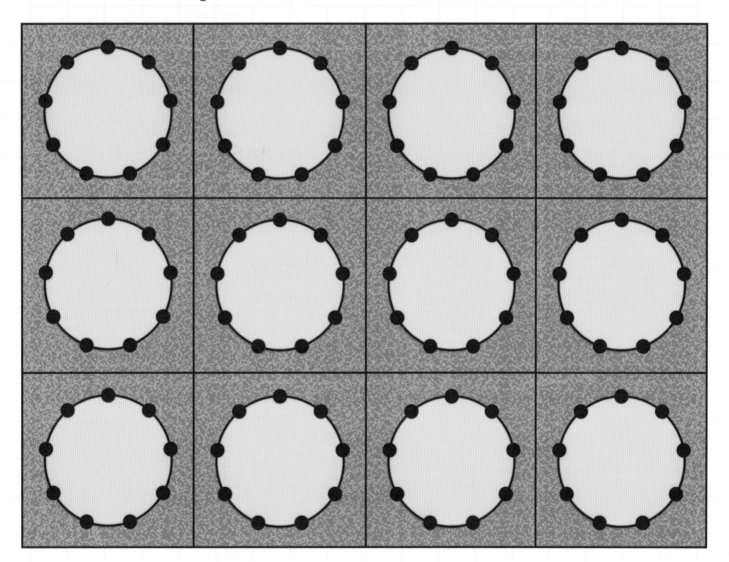

6D Drawing angles, and angles in a triangle

I. Find three reflex angles, three acute angles and three obtuse angles in your classroom.

- Measure your angles using your angle measurer and a protractor.
- List your angles in ascending order in this table:

Type of angle	Location	Angle size

2. Find four different triangles in your classroom.

- Measure the angles.
- What do you notice about the sum of the angles in each of your triangles?
- Use the angles to draw accurate sketches of your triangles:

6 Shapes and geometry

You want to design a new playground for the local kindergarten.

In your playground include: a balance beam, a climbing frame, swings and a hopscotch game.

Tasks:

1. Design the balance beam.

   What is the best 3D shape to use for the balance beam?

   Think about how to make the beam stable.

   What angles will you use?

2. What shapes will you include in the climbing frame?

3. Design a hopscotch game.

   Use at least three different 2D shapes.

4. Make a 3D model of the swings.

   Think about how to make the swings stable.

   What angles will you use?

5. Draw a sketch of the playground to illustrate your results:

6 Shapes and geometry

- Find at least two 2D and two 3D shapes in your classroom.
- Draw them in the table below.
- Write clues so that your friends can guess what the objects are.

Photo or drawing of object	Clues
	I. 2. 3. 4. 5.
	I. 2. 3. 4. 5.
	I. 2. 3. 4. 5.
	I. 2. 3. 4. 5.
	I. 2. 3. 4. 5.

7 Position and Movement

Engage

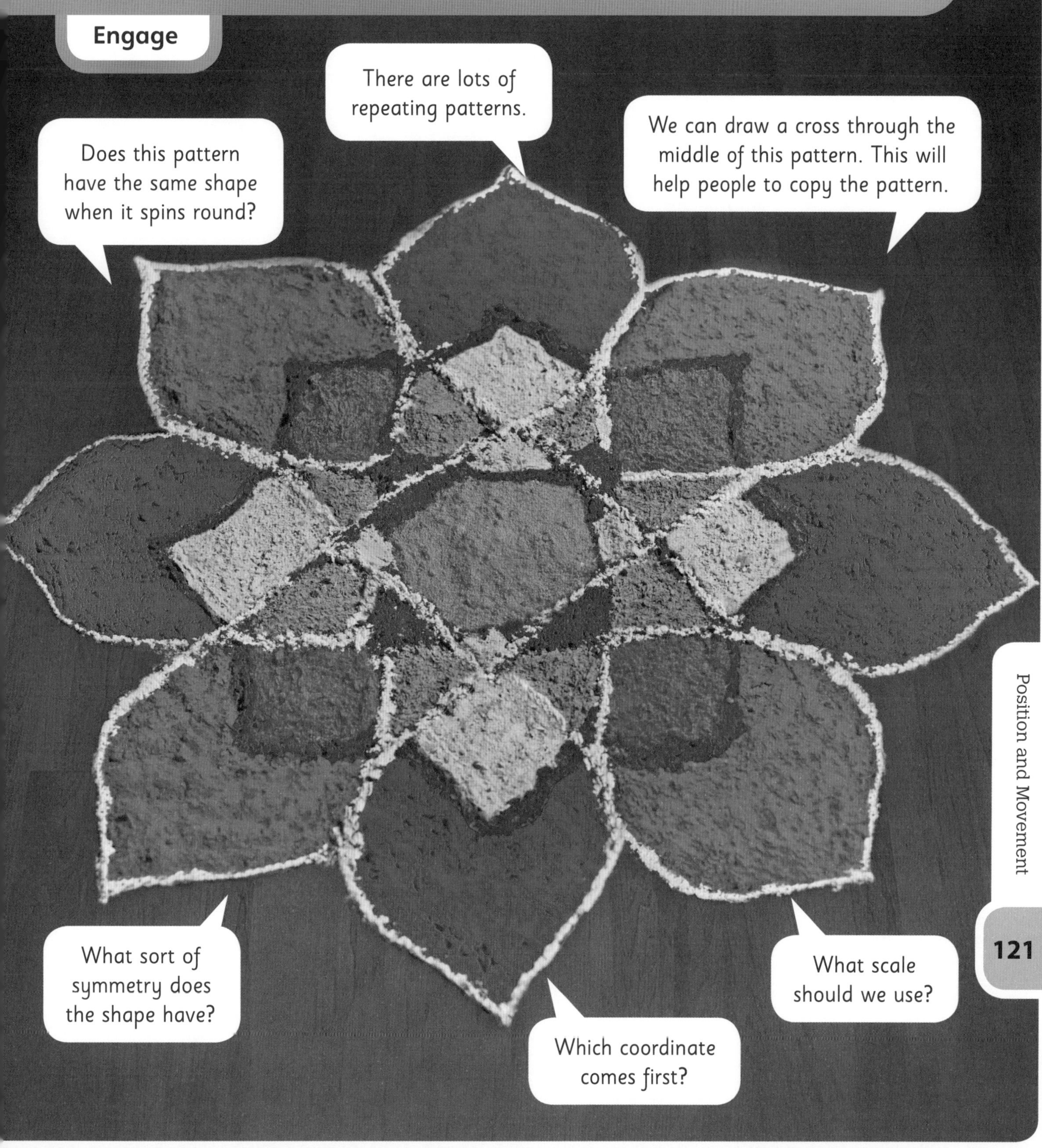

7A Reading and plotting coordinates

Discover

- Draw a plan of your classroom on the **coordinate** grid below. How can you find the centre of the classroom?

- Place the centre of the classroom at the **origin** (0, 0).

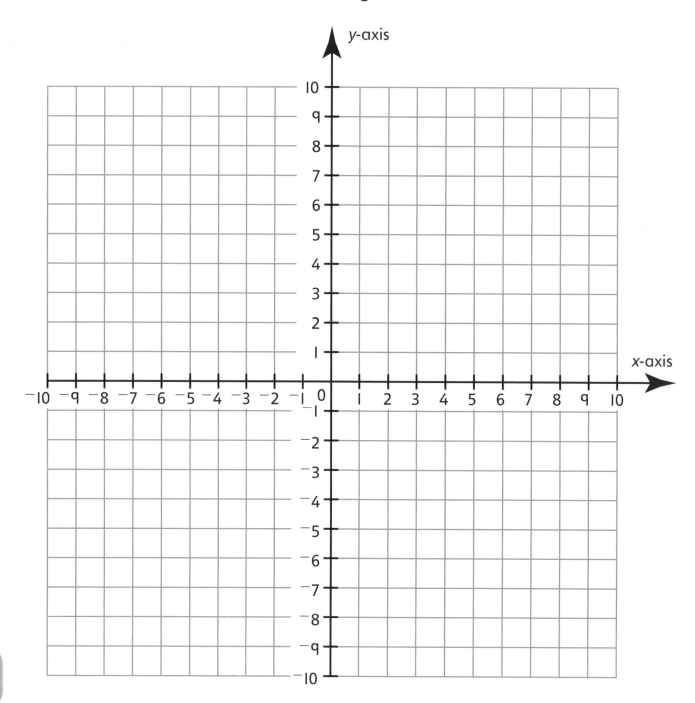

- Write five statements about the position of people or objects in your classroom. In your statements use coordinates in all four **quadrants**.

For example:
Sohm is sitting at ($^-$**3, 2**).
The teacher's desk is at (**0, 5**).

1.

2.

3.

4.

5.

Explore

I. Draw a different polygon in each grid so that each polygon has a **vertex** in each quadrant.

- Label the **vertices** with their coordinates.

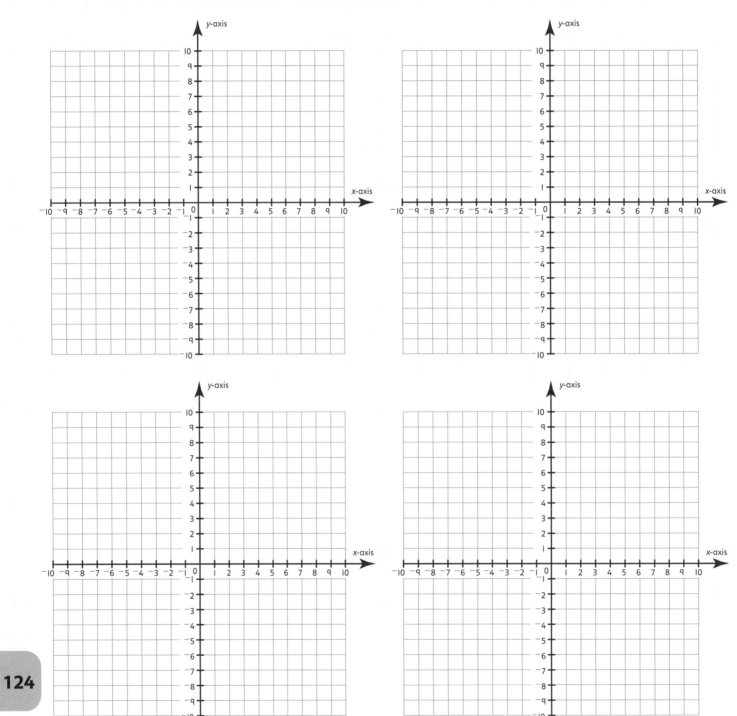

2. Work with a partner.

- Give your partner the coordinates for your shapes from question I.
- Ask your partner to use the coordinates to draw the shapes in their grids.
- Ask your partner to write the name of the shape under each grid.
- Follow your partner's instructions to draw shapes on the grids below.

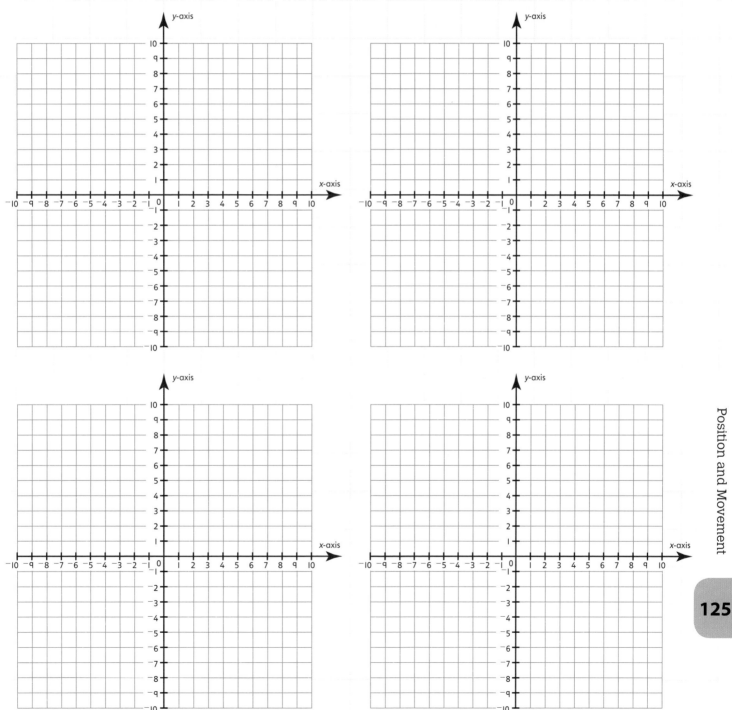

Discover

Look at this piece of art:

- Write down all the **reflections**, **rotations** or **translations** that you can see:

- Make a piece of art.
  Include shapes that are **reflected**, **translated** and **rotated**.

7B Reflections and rotations

Explore

- Draw a simple shape on a piece of card. For example:

- Cut your shape out.

- Place your shape on the grid, with one straight edge against the y-axis:

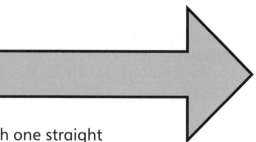

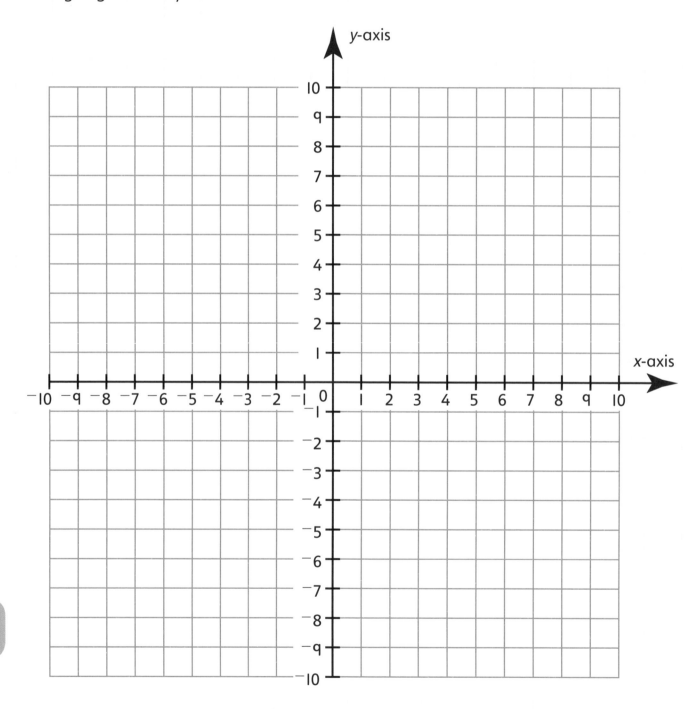

- Write down the coordinates of each vertex:

    1.   2.   3.

    4.   5.   6.

    7.   8.   9.

1. Slide the shape across the grid to a new position:
    Write down the new coordinates of each vertex:

    1.   2.   3.

    4.   5.   6.

    7.   8.   9.

2. Rotate the original shape clockwise through 90° about one vertex:
    Write down the new coordinates:

    1.   2.   3.

    4.   5.   6.

    7.   8.   9.

3. Reflect the original shape about the x-axis:
    Write down the new coordinates:

    1.   2.   3.

    4.   5.   6.

    7.   8.   9.

7 Position and movement

Look at the logos below:

- Design a logo for your school.
- Use repeated simple shapes.
- Draw your logo on the grid below so that it is easy to reproduce:

7 Position and movement

- Design a poster to explain all the important terms from this Unit. You and your friends can use this poster to remember these terms.
- Include images to illustrate the meanings of the following terms:

origin	coordinates
quadrants	line of symmetry
axis of symmetry	mirror line
reflection	translation
rotation	clockwise
anti-clockwise	

8 Length, Mass and Capacity

8A Selecting and using appropriate units of measure

Discover

I. Complete this table.

Write down objects that you can use these units to measure:

Unit	Object
kilometre	
metre	
centimetre	
millimetre	
tonne	
kilogram	
gram	
milligram	
litre	
centilitre	
millitre	

2. Sometimes we use different units of measure called 'Imperial units'.

> **(Miles)**
>
> In the USA they use miles to measure distance.
>
> A **kilometre** is $\frac{5}{8}$ of a mile.

Write similar sentences which include the following units:

a) **(Feet)**

_____

_____

b) **(Inches)**

_____

_____

c) **(Pounds)**

_____

_____

d) **(Ounces)**

_____

_____

e) **(Pints)**

_____

_____

3. In a group, choose an animal and find out facts about it.

- Prepare a presentation.
- Include the following information:

The animal **weighs**...

The animal has a **length** of...

The animal can run/fly/swim at a speed of...

8A Selecting and using appropriate units of measure

Explore

I. Draw a line to connect each description to the correct **measurement** on the right.

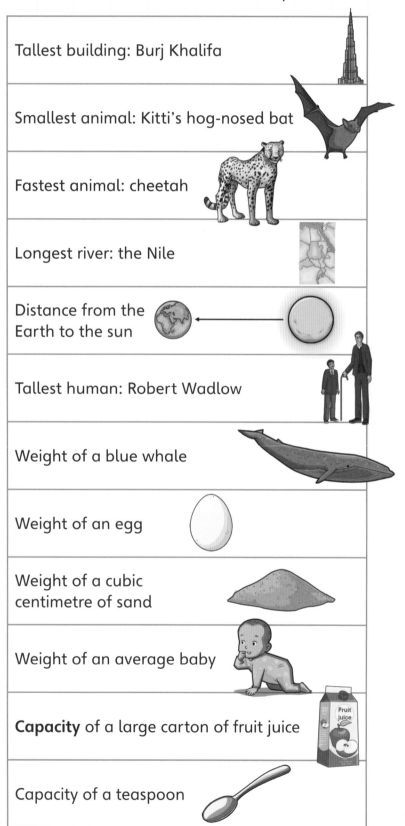

Tallest building: Burj Khalifa	65 km per hour
Smallest animal: Kitti's hog-nosed bat	6650 km
Fastest animal: cheetah	149 600 000 km
Longest river: the Nile	830 m high
Distance from the Earth to the sun	3.4 kg
Tallest human: Robert Wadlow	3 cm long
Weight of a blue whale	5 ml
Weight of an egg	1 litre
Weight of a cubic centimetre of sand	53 g
Weight of an average baby	190 tonnes
Capacity of a large carton of fruit juice	2.6 g
Capacity of a teaspoon	2.34 m

2. Write a sentence for each fact.
   Include a comparison.

The height of Burj Khalifa is about the same distance as two laps round an athletics track.

A baby weighs about the same as 1000 cubic centimetres of sand.

8B Converting units of measurement

Discover

- Work in pairs.
- Convert the **units of measure** and complete the tables.
- Find an object, or think of an object, as an example for each measurement.

1. Length

Metres	Centimetres	Millimetres	Object
		1 mm	
		10 mm	
		34.5 mm	
	50.7 cm		
	75 cm		
0.855 m			
10.3 m			
150 m			

2. Capacity

Litres	Centilitres	Millilitres	Object
		3.2 ml	
		8 ml	
		57.8 ml	
	25.9 cl		
	68.7 cl		
0.55 litres			
15.2 litres			
50 litres			

3. Weight

Kilograms	Grams	Milligrams	Object
	0.5 g		
	0.85 g		
		220 mg	
		325 mg	
0.050 kg			
0.750 kg			
22.5 kg			
175.5 kg			

What did you notice about converting between units?

I noticed that when you convert from _____ to _____ you _____.

8B Converting units of measurement

Explore

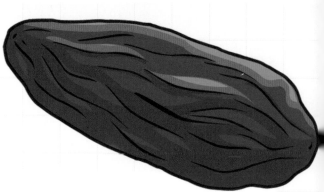

1. The width of a currant is approximately 3 mm.

   How many currants can you fit on the length of:

   a) your desk _____

   b) your classroom _____

2. 100 g of uncooked lentils contains 25 g of protein.

   How much do you weigh (in grams)?

   _____

   How much protein does your bodyweight
   of lentils contain?

   _____

3. A can of fizzy drink has a capacity of 25 centilitres.
   A **gallon** is approximately 4.5 litres

   How many cans of fizzy drink fill a jug with a
   capacity of 1 gallon?

   _____

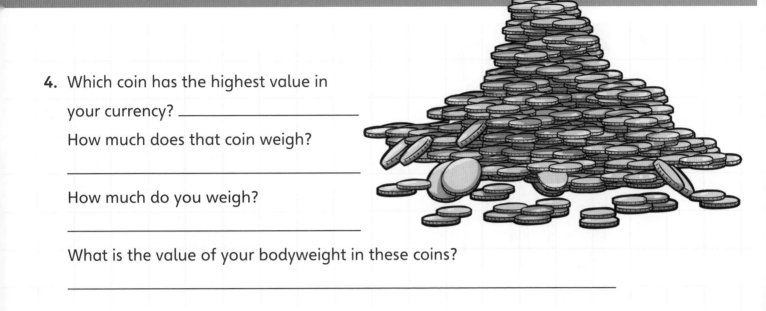

4. Which coin has the highest value in
your currency? _____

How much does that coin weigh?

_____

How much do you weigh?

_____

What is the value of your bodyweight in these coins?

_____

5. What is the distance between your home and
the school? _____

• Measure the length of your stride.
Your stride is the distance you travel in one step.

_____

_____

How many strides would it take to walk from your
home to your school?

_____

_____

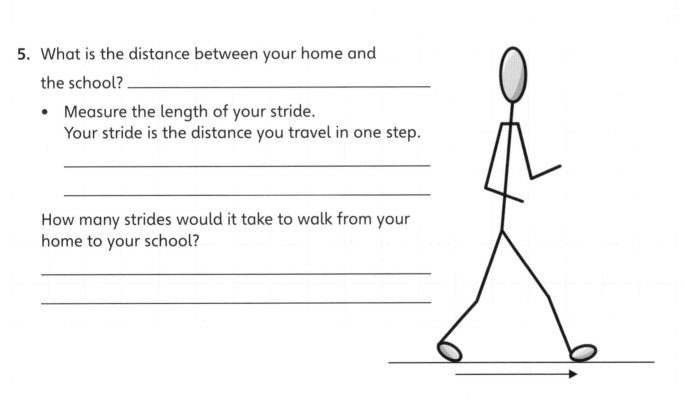

8C Using scales and measuring accurately

Discover

I think that my height is 4 times the circumference of my head.

Is this true?

• Use this table to record your measurements:

Height	Circumference of head	Height ÷ circumference of head

I discovered that your height is approximately ☐ times the circumference of your head.

8C Using scales and measuring acurately

Explore

1.

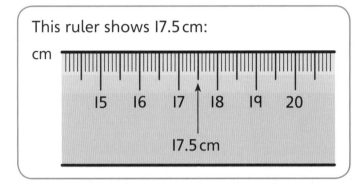

This ruler shows 17.5 cm:

- Mark each of these rulers to show the measurement:

   a) 28 cm

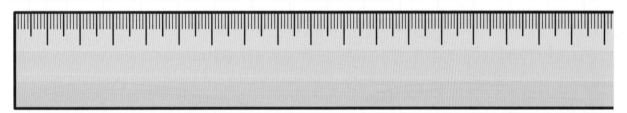

   b) 4.5 cm

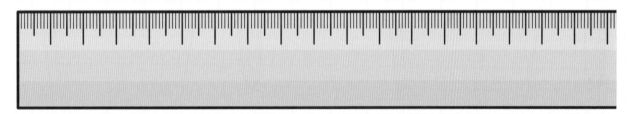

   c) 0.5 cm

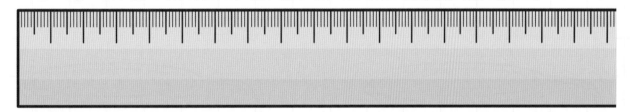

   d) 11.5 cm

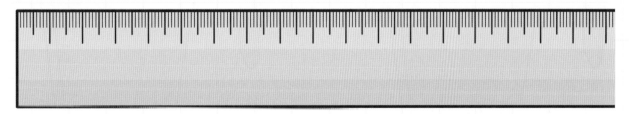

Length, Mass and Capacity

2.

This measuring jug shows 630 ml:

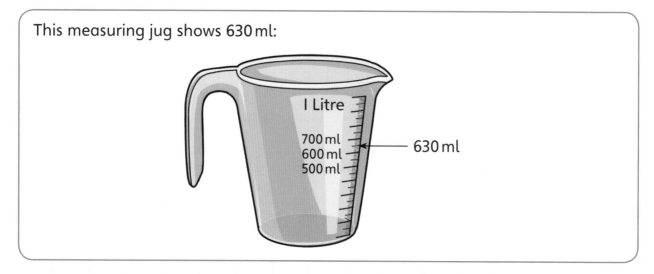

700 ml — 600 ml — 500 ml — → 630 ml

- Mark each of these measuring jugs to show the measure:

a) 170 ml

c) 35 ml

b) 890 ml

d) 250 ml

3.

This scale shows 825 g:

825 g ←

- Mark these scales to show the weights:

a) 950 g

b) 15 g

c) 520 g

d) 430 g

4. Draw lines next to these measurements:
Draw your lines accurate **to the nearest millimetre**.

a) 10.7 cm

b) 5.3 cm

c) 1.2 cm

d) 15.8 cm

e) 12.5 cm

8 Length, mass and capacity

You are working for a pie-making company.

The pastry rolling machine rolls out rectangles of pastry that measure 1 m by 75 cm.

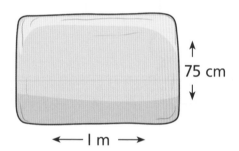

75 cm

←— 1 m —→

The circular base of a pie has a diameter of 8 cm.

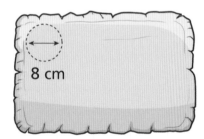

8 cm

The circular top of a pie has a diameter of 4 cm.

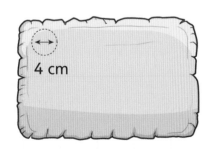

4 cm

How can you cut the pastry to make the maximum number of pies?

Draw a diagram to show your solution:

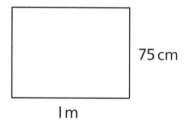

75 cm

1 m

A pie contains 25 ml of filling.

The filling is sold in jars of 250 ml.

How much filling do you need to fill all of the pies you make?

_____

How many jars of filling do you need

to buy? _____

8 Length, mass and capacity

- Colour the boxes with matching measures in the same colour.
- Fill in the empty boxes with two new sets of matching measures.

2.5 m	$\frac{7}{10}$ litre	2.4 kg	
0.6 kg		$\frac{1}{4}$ litre	$2\frac{1}{2}$ m
250 ml	0.015 litre	600 000 mg	
	2.5 m	0.02 m	700 ml
0.7 litre		1.5 cl	0.25 litre
2400 g		$2\frac{2}{5}$ kg	250 cm
2 cm	600 g		
15 ml			20 mm

9 Time

I sleep for **8** hours a night. How many hours will I sleep for in my whole life?

It is impossible to live for a million seconds.

How many hours will I spend in school in total?

It is always night-time somewhere in the world.

I can think of **10** different clocks or timers I see in a normal day.

How many minutes have there been so far this year?

Discover

I. On a **digital 24-hour clock**, at certain times, all the digits are consecutive.

The same times shown on an **analogue clock**:

How many times like this are there between:

a) 23:00 and 05:00? _____

• Record your answers as **analogue times** and **digital times**:

b) 09:00 and 13:00? _____

 • Record your answers as analogue times and digital times:

c) **midday** and **midnight**?

 • Record your answers as analogue times and digital times:

9A Converting between units of time

Explore

1. Complete this table:

Number of **centuries** in a **millennium**	
Number of **decades** in a century	
Number of **years** in a decade	10
Number of **months** in a year	
Number of **weeks** in a year	
Number of **days** in a week	7
Number of **hours** in a day	
Number of **minutes** in an hour	
Number of **seconds** in a minute	
Number of **milliseconds** in a second	

- Use the information in the table to answer these questions:

2. How many days old are you?

3. How many seconds have there been in this year so far?

4. How many milliseconds are there in a maths lesson?

5. Pick 3 different historical events. How many decades ago did they happen?

6. It is 2014 seconds after the start of 2014. What day is it? What time is it?

7. Find a friend who is younger than you. How many days older than them are you?

8. What date is 1 million days after the start of this millennium?

9. How many weeks are there in this century?

9B Using the 24-hour clock and timetables

Discover

- Complete these **timetables**.
- Use the **24-hour clock**.
- Use each timetable to write down five facts.

For example: Lunchtime is from 12:30 to 13:30.

1. **A school day**

a) _____

b) _____

c) _____

d) _____

e) _____

2. **A holiday**

a) _____

b) _____

c) _____

d) _____

e) _____

3. **A school trip**

a) _____

b) _____

c) _____

d) _____

e) _____

Explore

You are the manager of a bus company.

You need to design a route for buses to bring students to your school and take them home.

There is also a community centre at your school.

The community centre offers classes that start at 11:00 and 13:00.

The last bus leaves the bus station at 19:30.

1. Draw a map below to show the route the bus will take.
   On your map include:

   • six different bus stops including the school and the bus station

   • the time taken between each stop

   • a circular route.

2. Now complete this timetable for the journeys:
   Your buses leave at 10 different times.

Bus Station										
Stop 1										
Stop 2										
Stop 3										
Stop 4										
Stop 5										
Bus Station										

Time

9C Calculating time intervals including time zones

Discover

- Look at this map of **international time zones** around the world:

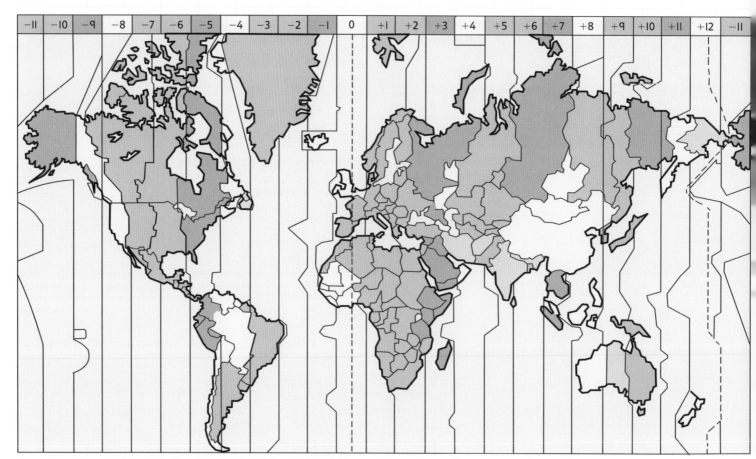

| −11 | −10 | −9 | −8 | −7 | −6 | −5 | −4 | −3 | −2 | −1 | 0 | +1 | +2 | +3 | +4 | +5 | +6 | +7 | +8 | +9 | +10 | +11 | +12 | −11 |

- Use this map to write down ten facts:

1. _____

2. _____

3. _____

4. _____

5. _____

6. _____

7. _____

8. _____

9. _____

10. _____

9C Calculating time intervals including time zones

Explore

1. What is the best time to telephone your friend in Australia?

_____

2. Your friend in California goes to bed at 22:20. What time is this where you live?

_____

3. You come home from school at 16:00. What time is this for your friend in the UK?

_____

4. Will your friend in Argentina celebrate New Year before or after you? _____
   By how many hours?

_____

5. Your class is twinned with a class in Madagascar.
   When is the best time to have a Skype conversation?

_____

6. a) Complete this table to show the times in different cities of the world.

   b) Add two cities that you would like to visit.

Home	00:00	02:00	04:00	06:00	08:00	10:00	12:00	14:00	16:00	18:00	20:00	22:00
New York												
Tokyo												
Sydney												
Cape Town												
Bangkok												

Time

c) You fly from New York to Tokyo.
    The flight takes 14 hours.
    It **departs** at 09:30.
    What time (local time) do you **arrive** in Tokyo?

    _____

    _____

    _____

    _____

    _____

    _____

d) You fly from Cape Town to Sydney.
    It takes 13 hours 45 minutes.
    You depart at 22:30.
    What time (local time) do you arrive in Sydney?

    _____

    _____

    _____

    _____

    _____

    _____

e) You fly from Sydney to Bangkok.
    The flight takes 9 hours 15 minutes.
    You depart from Sydney at 13:15.
    What time (local time) do you arrive in Bangkok?

    _____

    _____

    _____

    _____

    _____

    _____

9 Time

Connect

You are planning a school trip to an island.
You cannot reach the island when the tide is high.
You cannot depart from school until 08:30.
You must be back at school by 19:30.
The journey to the coast takes 45 minutes.
You want to spend at least 4 hours on the island.
You have four possible dates to choose from for the trip.

This timetable shows the times when the tide is high:

5 July	08:00–10:00	15:00–17:00
12 July	10:00–12:00	17:00–19:00
19 July	12:00–14:00	19:00–21:00
26 July	14:00–16:00	21:00–23:00

1. How long can you spend on the island on each of these days?

   _____

   _____

   _____

   _____

2. Which is the best day for your school trip? _____

   • Write the timetable below.

3. Why is this the best day for the trip?

   _____

   _____

9 Time

- Write five questions to test your friends on what they have learned during this Unit.
- Include a solution for each method and illustrate the method.

I. Telling the time on analogue and digital clocks

   a) _____

   b) _____

   c) _____

   d) _____

   e) _____

2. Converting between units of time

   a) _____

   b) _____

   c) _____

   d) _____

   e) _____

3. Using the 24-hour clock

   a) _____

   b) _____

   c) _____

   d) _____

   e) _____

4. Using timetables

a) _____

b) _____

c) _____

d) _____

e) _____

5. Using international time zones

a) _____

b) _____

c) _____

d) _____

e) _____

10 Area and Perimeter

Every shape with a perimeter of **24** cm has the same area.

I double the perimeter. The new area is always double the original area.

There are lots of different shapes with the same area.

Every shape with the area **16** cm² has the same perimeter.

I don't think that is always true.

Discover

A farmer has 24 metres of wire fencing.

He wants to enclose the maximum possible **area** of land to allow his goats to graze.

What shape of area do you advise him to enclose?

- Investigate a range of rectangles and other **rectilinear** shapes like these:

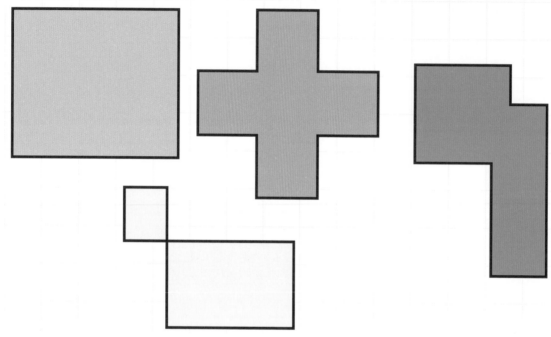

10A Area and perimeter of rectilinear shapes

Rectilinear shapes are not just rectangles.

Here are some examples:

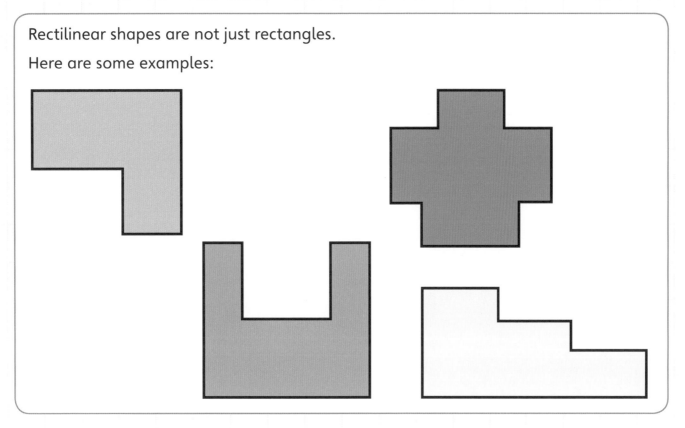

- Draw two different rectilinear shapes with the following areas.
- Write the **perimeter** under each shape.

I. Area of 36 cm²

2. Area of 68 cm²

4. Area of 250 cm²

3. Area of 125 cm²

5. Area of 360 cm²

Discover

- On the squared paper below draw round your open hand.
- Count the squares to find the area.

- Complete this table.
- Use 15 other students' measurements.

The hand length is from the top of the wrist to the tip of the middle finger.

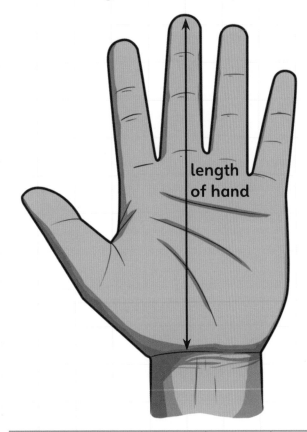

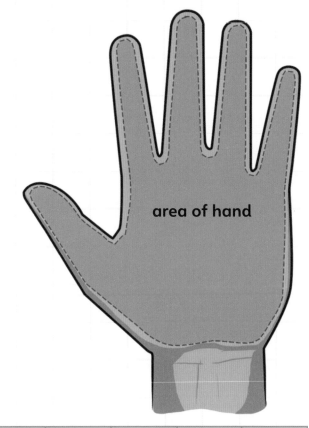

Friend's name							
Area of hand							
Length of hand							
Friend's name							
Area of hand							
Length of hand							

- Use the squared paper below.
- Draw a **scattergram** of area against length.

Is there any **correlation**?

Explore

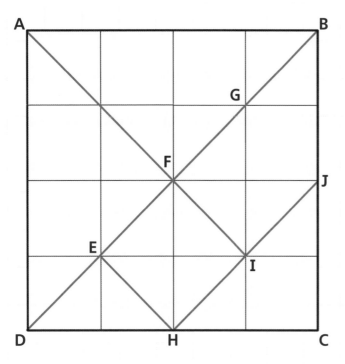

- Write the area of each piece of the tangram on the diagram above.
- Sketch five different shapes using pieces of the tangram:
- I. An arrangement using three pieces:

2. An arrangement using four pieces:

4. A different arrangement using five pieces:

3. An arrangement using five pieces:

5. An arrangement using six pieces:

• Write the area and perimeter under each shape.

Discover

You can represent data in different ways so that it is easier to understand.

The example below shows an example of a three-country continent.

The countries all share a border with each other. They are surrounded by sea.

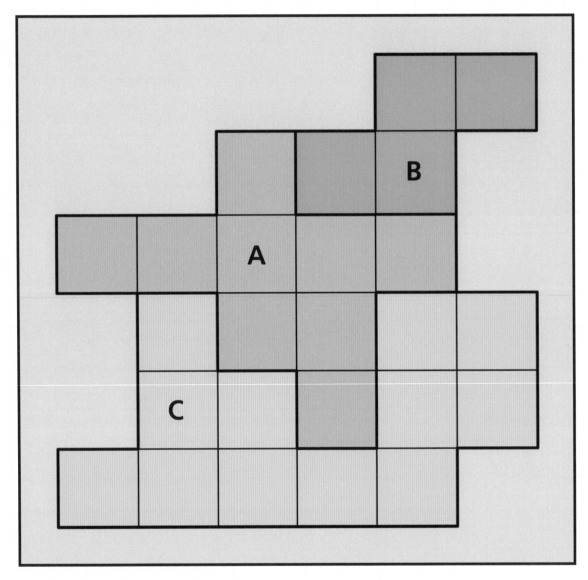

In this view, the areas of countries A, B and C are shown as 18, 8 and 24 million km² (so each square represents 2 million km²).

- Draw a new view of these countries to show different information.
- Represent countries A, B and C as having populations of 40, 36 and 24 million people.

Make sure that you can recognise each country and its position.
Keep the shapes and positions of the countries relative to each other as similar to the original as possible.

Explore

You work for a company that sells stock cubes.

You sell the stock cubes in packs of 12, 24, 40 and 100.

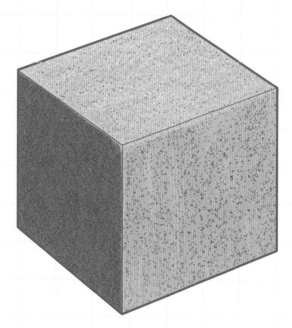

1 stock cube is a 2 cm cube.

- Use cubes to model the size of the boxes that you need to make to hold the stock cubes.

- Include two different possibilities for each.

- Sketch the nets of each of the boxes below.

- Under each net write the **surface area** (total area of net) and the perimeter.

1. Nets for 12 cubes:

a)

b)

2. Nets for 24 cubes:

a) b)

3. Nets for 40 cubes:

a) b)

4. Nets for 100 cubes:

a) b)

10 Area and perimeter

- Draw a scale drawing of your classroom below:

You decide to buy four cupboards.

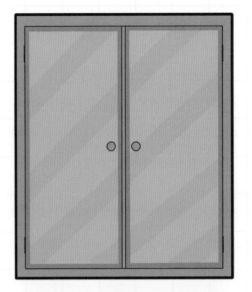

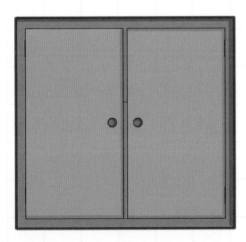

The dimensions of their bases are:

A: 1.5 m by 0.5 m

B: 2 m by 0.75 m

C: 1 m by 0.75 m

D: 2.5 m by 0.5 m

- Decide where you want to put the cupboards in the room.
- Draw them onto your scale plan.

You want to tile the classroom floor using three different colours of tile.

All tiles are squares of side 0.5m. They cost:

blue tiles $20 per square metre

red tiles $25 per square metre

patterned tiles $32 per square metre

- Draw three different designs for the classroom floor.
- Work out the cost for each design.

Design 1

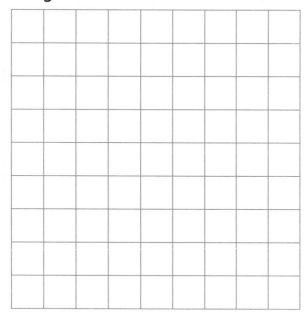

Design 3

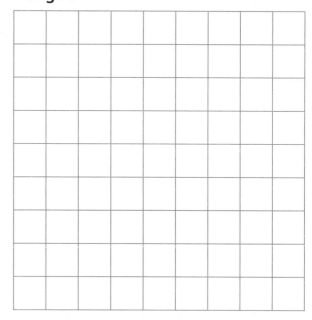

Design 2

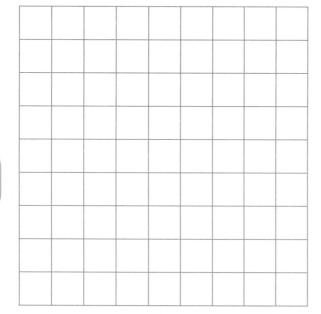

10 Area and perimeter

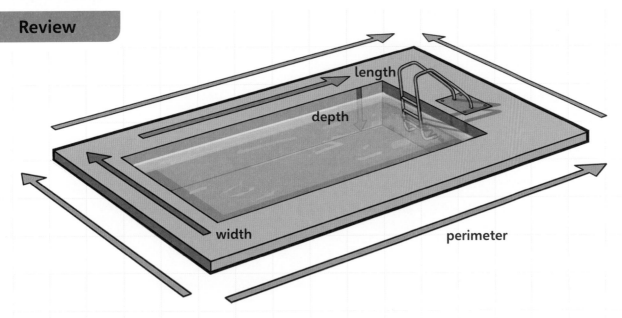

- Use the box below to sketch ideas for a poster.

- In your poster explain the key terms from this Unit.

- Draw pictures and label them with the following words:

  length, width, height, depth, breadth

  edge, perimeter, circumference

  area, surface, face

  square centimetre (cm²), square metre (m²), square millimetre (mm²)

11 Handling Data

What is the climate like here compared to other countries?

How many languages do students speak in our school? How does this compare to other schools?

How do children travel to my school? Is this the same as schools in other places?

How can we encourage people to be more environmentally friendly?

When is the best time to have school holidays?

1, 2, 3, 4...

Are women's times getting closer to men's times in sprint races?

Defining my question

What are we interested in finding out?
List all your ideas here:

Pick one question you are particularly interested in and write it here:

11A Handling data

What do I know already?

Our question is:

_____

_____

Source	Information we found out

Carrying out a survey

Our **survey** question is:

_____

_____

These are questions that we will ask people:

1. _____
2. _____
3. _____
4. _____
5. _____
6. _____
7. _____
8. _____

We are asking the following people:

Group	Number of people asked	Reason for asking this group of people

These are the results of our survey listed in a **frequency table**:

Representing the data

Here are our results.

We used a _____ because _____

_____

We chose not to use a _____ because

_____

11A Handling data

Interpreting the data – planning a presentation

Our question is:

_____

_____

Our reason for asking this question

We wanted to ask this question because:

What we found out from research

Our research showed us that:

What we found out from our survey

We found out from our survey that:

What we found out

So, we now know that:

Another question we would like to ask based on our findings

Now we would like to ask this question:

11B Probability

Discover

- Play the Great Horse Race game with your friends.

Horse										Winning post
1										
2										
3										
4										
5										
6										
7										
8										
9										
10										
11										
12										

You play the game again. Which horse do you choose as a winner?

_____

Why do you choose this horse? _____

_____

Which horse do you definitely not choose? _____

Why do you definitely not choose this horse? _____

_____

What is the probability that horse number 5 wins?

11B Probability

Explore

1. Complete this table:

Chosen outcome	Equally likely outcomes	Number of possible required outcomes	Probability fraction	Probability as percentage
Rolling an even number on a 6-sided dice	I can roll 1, 2, 3, 4, 5 or 6	There are 3 even numbers (2, 4, 6)	There are 3 chances out of 6 so the probability is $\frac{3}{6}$ (or $\frac{1}{2}$)	$\frac{1}{2}$ is the same as 50%
Rolling an even total on two 6-sided dice				
Rolling a number less than 4 on a 10-sided dice				
Picking a 7 or a 9 out of a pack of cards				
Picking a Jack, Queen or King out of a pack of cards				

2. Write down events with the following probabilities:

a) $\frac{1}{2}$

_____

_____

_____

b) 0 (impossible)

_____

_____

_____

c) $\frac{2}{5}$

_____

_____

_____

d) $\frac{1}{10}$

_____

_____

_____

e) 90%

_____

_____

_____

f) 1 (**certain** to happen)

_____

_____

_____

arc

_____

_____

_____

arcs

average

_____

_____

_____

Here are five numbers ranging from 3 to 9:

3 3 4 6 9

The **mean** is 5 because. $\frac{3+3+4+6+9}{5} = 5$

The **median** is 4 because it is the middle value.

The **mode** is 3 because it occurs most often.

biased

_____

_____

_____

centilitre

_____

_____

_____

100 **centilitres** = 1 litre

100 **cl** = 1 l

1 **cl** = 10 ml

1 **centilitre** = $\frac{1}{100}$ litre

circumference

_____

_____

circumference ⟶

common multiple

_____

_____

12 is a **common multiple** of 3 and 4. It is also a common multiple of 6 and 2.

composite number

_____

_____

_____

18 is a **composite number** because it can be written as 3×6 or 2×9.

3 and 7 are not composite numbers.

concentric

_____

_____

_____

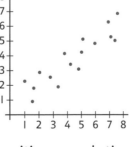   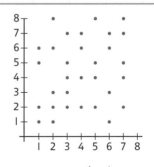

concentric circles   **concentric** squares

correlation

_____

_____

_____

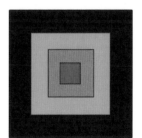

positive correlation   no correlation

cross-section

_____

_____

_____

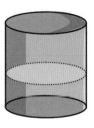

The **cross-section** of a cylinder is a circle.

decade

_____

_____

_____

I **decade** = 10 years

10 **decades** = 1 century

decimal equivalent

_____

_____

_____

Here are some **decimal equivalents**:

$\frac{1}{10} = 0.1 \qquad \frac{2}{10} = 0.2 \qquad \frac{4}{100} = 0.04$

directed numbers

_____

_____

_____

_____

negative numbers   positive numbers

−4 −3 −2 −1   0   1   2   3   4

dividend

_____

_____

_____

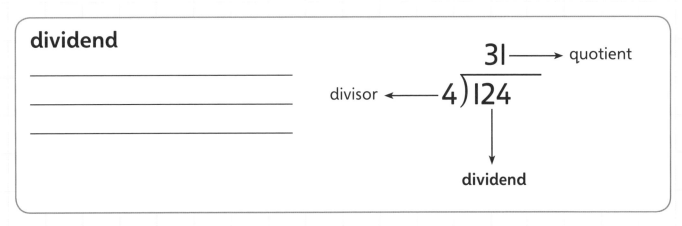

$$31 \longrightarrow \text{quotient}$$

$$\text{divisor} \longleftarrow 4\overline{)124}$$

dividend

divisor

_____

_____

_____

$$31 \longrightarrow \text{quotient}$$

$$\text{divisor} \longleftarrow 4\overline{)124}$$

dividend

dodecahedron

_____

_____

_____

regular dodecahedron

equal chance (even chance, fifty-fifty chance)

_____

_____

_____

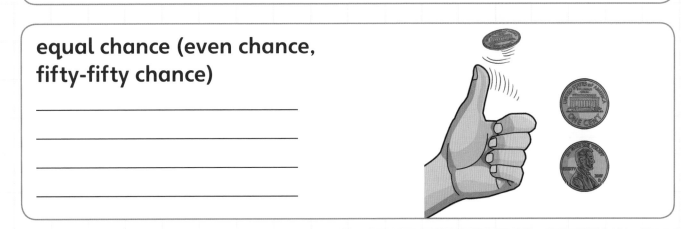

equally likely

_____
_____
_____
_____

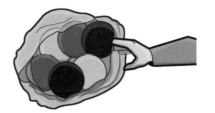

event

_____
_____
_____
_____
_____

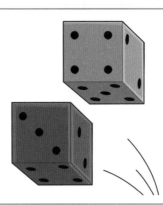

factorise

_____
_____
_____

$$42 = 2 \times 3 \times 7$$

Factorising the number 42.

foot (plural feet)

_____
_____
_____

1 **foot** = 12 inches

3 **feet** = 1 yard

1 **foot** = 30.48 cm

front elevation

_____

_____

_____

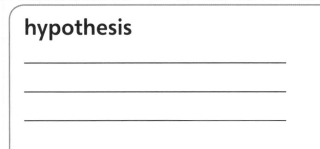

front elevation

hypothesis

_____

_____

_____

identical

_____

_____

_____

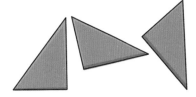

Identical shapes can be in different positions.

inch (plural inches)

_____

_____

_____

12 **inches** = 1 foot

1 **inch** = 2.54 cm

interior angle

_____

_____

_____

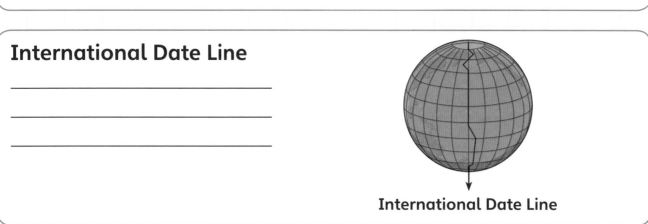

interior angle ←

International Date Line

_____

_____

_____

International Date Line

international time zones

_____

_____

_____

II a.m. New York   5 p.m. Rome

7 p.m. Riyadh

intersect

_____

_____

_____

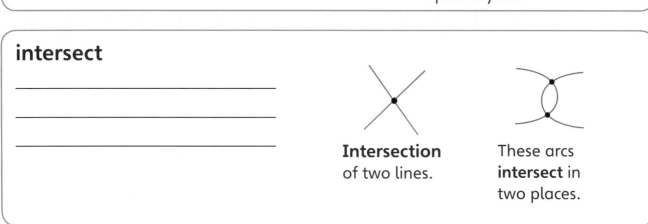

Intersection of two lines.

These arcs **intersect** in two places.

kite

_____

_____

_____

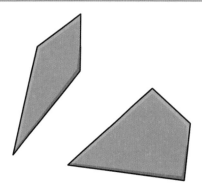

mean

_____

_____

_____

Here are five numbers ranging from 3 to 9:

3   3   4   6   9

The total is $\frac{3 + 3 + 4 + 6 + 9}{5} = \frac{25}{5} = 5$.

The **mean** is _____.

median

_____

_____

_____

_____

Here are five numbers ranging from 3 to 9:

3   3   4   6   9

The **median** is 4 because it is the middle value.

operation key

_____

_____

_____

operation keys

ounce (oz) (plural ounces)

_____

_____

_____

16 **ounces** = 1 pound

16 oz = 1 lb

1 **ounce** = 28.3 grams

parallelogram

_____

_____

_____

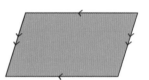

The arrowheads show which sides of the **parallelogram** are parallel to each other.

plan view

_____

_____

_____

plan view

plane

_____

_____

_____

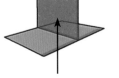

vertical **plane**

horizontal **plane**

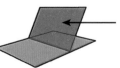

oblique **plane**

pound (lb)

_____

_____

_____

1 **pound** = 16 ounces

1 **lb** = 16 oz

1 **lb** = 453.59 g

1 kg = 2.204 **lb**

prime factor

_____

_____

_____

The factors of 24 are 1, 2, 3, 4, 6, 8, 12, 24.

The **prime factors** of 24 are 2 and 3.

prime number

_____

_____

_____

These are the **prime numbers** less than 20.

random

_____

_____

_____

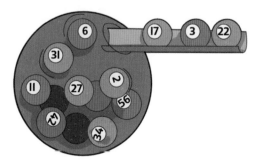

rectilinear

_____

_____

_____

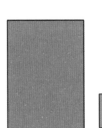

rectilinear shapes

recurring

_____

_____

_____

Some **recurring** decimals:

$\frac{1}{3}$ = 0.333333333333 →

This number is called 'zero point three **recurring**'.

$\frac{22}{7}$ = 3.1428561428561 →

The digits 142856 keep repeating.

reflex angle

_____

_____

_____

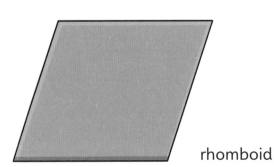

reflex angles

rhomboid

_____

_____

_____

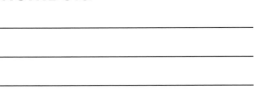

rhomboid

rhombus

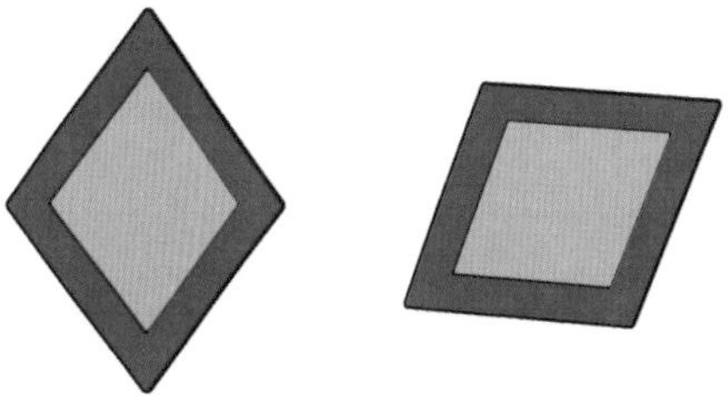

_____
_____
_____

rhombus

side elevation

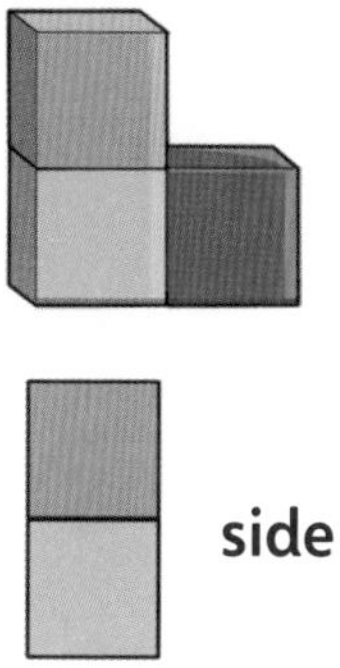

_____
_____
_____

side elevation

symmetry

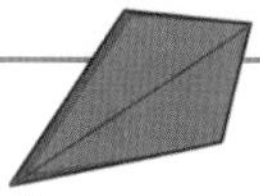

_____
_____
_____
_____

A kite has **symmetry** about a line.

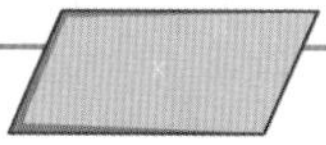

A parallelogram has rotational **symmetry** about a point.

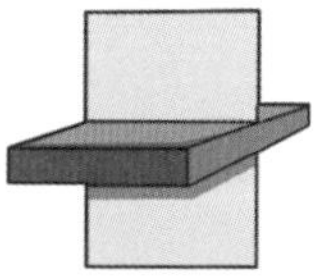

A cuboid has **symmetry** about a plane.

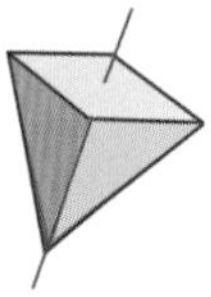

A pyramid has rotational **symmetry** about an axis.

tangram

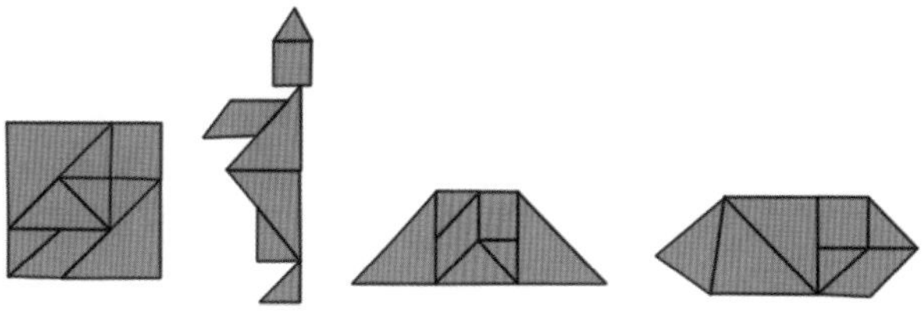

_____
_____
_____
_____

a **tangram** puzzle

tonne

_____

_____

_____

1 **tonne** = 1000 kilograms

1 **tonne** = 100 kg

transformation

_____

_____

_____

rotation

translation

reflection

trapezium

_____

_____

_____

trapezium

right-angled **trapezium**

isosceles **trapezium**

yard

_____

_____

_____

1 **yard** = 3 feet

1 **yard** = 36 inches

1 **yard** = 91.44 cm